I0572534

Editor's Picks

Caged

CC ROBINSON

A gripping, fast-paced dystopian sequel with high stakes, compelling characters, and relentless tension—Caged keeps readers hooked from start to finish.

Kindle: £3.89

https://tinyurl.com/yeyta4jj

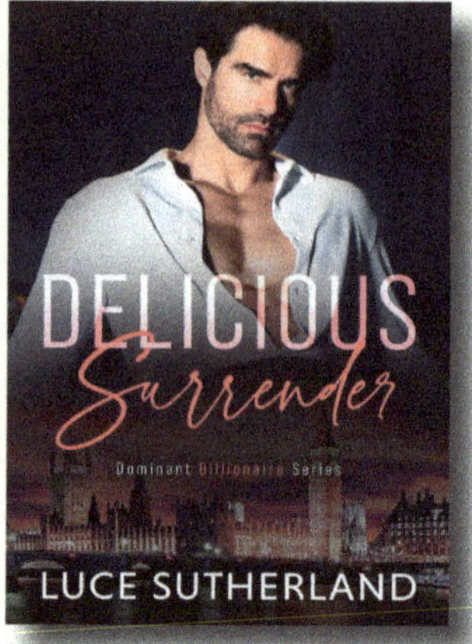

Delicious Surrender

LUCE SUTHERLAND

Intensely passionate, thrillingly suspenseful, and irresistibly steamy—Delicious Surrender delivers fiery chemistry, gripping tension, and a deeply satisfying romance.

Paperback: £13.99

https://tinyurl.com/mtty5fej

Henchmen

MATTHEW HUGHES

A gripping, witty fantasy adventure with rich world-building, engaging characters, and masterful storytelling—Hughes delivers intrigue, action, and unforgettable magic.

Paperback: £16.13

https://tinyurl.com/2wbe6ewn

The House Filler

TONG GE

A beautifully written, emotionally powerful novel that captures resilience, love, and survival amidst the turmoil of war and political unrest.

Paperback: £19.83

https://tinyurl.com/t2n5by5t

From Green to Blue

JONATHAN COX

Authentic, witty, and deeply human—Cox delivers a masterclass in storytelling that captures the heart and grit of real policing.

Paperback: £9.99

https://tinyurl.com/54yrxfbs

The Troubleseeker

ALAN LESSIK

A bold, lyrical journey blending myth and memory—The Troubleseeker is a masterful, moving tale of love and liberation.

Paperback: £12.99

https://tinyurl.com/3trwwtxy

That Last Carolina Summer

KAREN WHITE

Karen White masterfully crafts an emotional narrative filled with rich characters, gripping mysteries, and the enduring power of family bonds.

Kindle: £14.99

https://tinyurl.com/5fd92d2y

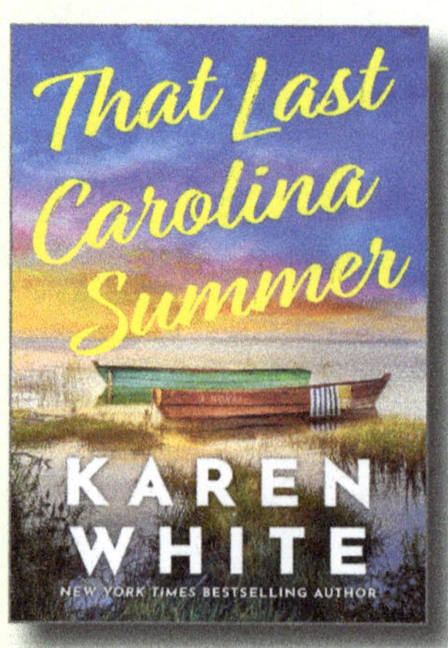

Sultry, Is the Night

BARBARA AVON

Barbara Avon's evocative prose, vivid imagery, and emotional depth make Sultry, Is the Night a hauntingly unforgettable read.

Paperback: £11.99

https://tinyurl.com/yvpf9ab9

Your Gateway to Endless Stories

Bewept

COLLEEN COYNE

Haunting, beautifully written, and deeply immersive. Bewept masterfully explores grief, memory, and suspense with poetic prose and psychological depth. Absolutely unforgettable.

Paperback: £14.99

https://tinyurl.com/tdwvup49

Deadside Reapers

DEBBIE CASSIDY

Thrilling, witty, and addictive! Deadside Reapers delivers sharp dialogue, intense action, and unforgettable characters in a brilliantly crafted urban fantasy world.

Paperback: £8.99

https://tinyurl.com/3hpxx8zk

Freedom Lessons

EILEEN H. SANCHEZ

A beautifully written, deeply immersive novel that masterfully blends history, faith, and suspense. Credito's storytelling is both poignant and unforgettable.

Paperback: £16.29

https://tinyurl.com/3rjszmk7

The Heart of a Soldier

ELEANOR ALSPAUGH

A deeply moving and impeccably researched tribute to courage, resilience, and love amidst the horrors of World War II.

Paperback: £19.66

https://tinyurl.com/yc58erpa

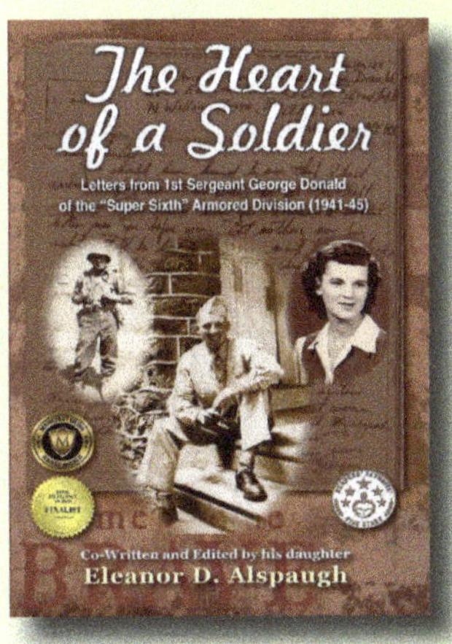

A Mother's Survival

HOPE BROOKS

Hope Brooks' memoir is a heartfelt, inspiring journey of resilience and strength, showcasing remarkable courage through life's toughest challenges.

Paperback: £5.91

https://tinyurl.com/25wztxtz

Lifting the Veil

KATE CHURCH

A beautifully written, emotionally rich fantasy that explores power, betrayal, and hope with unforgettable characters and masterful storytelling. A gripping triumph.

Paperback: £12.58

https://tinyurl.com/rszejjzb

A Sinful Temptation

KELLY BOYCE

Captivating, passionate, and beautifully written—A Sinful Temptation is a delightful blend of romance, mystery, and irresistible chemistry. Utterly enchanting!

Paperback: £15.26

https://tinyurl.com/3dks2z7v

Harvard

KIRSTEN PURSELL

Harvard by Kirsten Pursell is a beautifully written, emotionally resonant novel with compelling characters and a richly detailed setting. Highly recommended!

Paperback: £7.65

https://tinyurl.com/3udvmtrj

VOICES OF LITERATURE

What's INSIDE

AUTHOR INTERVIEWS

What's INSIDE

What's INSIDE

Issue 52 -2025

Scan QR to read online or updated issue.

From the Editor

Welcome to another exciting issue of Reader's House magazine! This edition, we are thrilled to shine the spotlight on A.M. Berkowitz, a beloved name in children's literature, whose enchanting stories have captivated young hearts and inspired imaginations across our vibrant reading community. As we feature Berkowitz on our cover, we invite you to dive into her magical world, where joy and creativity are cherished companions in every tale.

Berkowitz's delightful works, such as her debut "*Ladybug Kisses – Besos De Mariquita*" and the charming "*Gigglet the Happy Little Piglet*" series, illuminate the pages with laughter, warmth, and invaluable life lessons. Her journey from the operatic stage to the heart of corporate life and ultimately to the realm of storytelling is a testament to the inspiring truth that it is never too late to follow one's passion and make a profound impact on the lives of others. Through her engaging narratives, Berkowitz not only entertains but also empowers young readers to navigate the world with empathy and positivity.

In our exclusive interview, we delve into her creative process, the motivations that led her to establish AMB Kids Books, and her vision for the future. Berkowitz's passion radiates through her words as she shares her mission to spark a lifelong love for literature, create relatable characters, and curate stories that foster emotional resilience. Her upcoming adventures, including Gigglet's new sibling story, promise to continue her legacy of joy-filled narratives.

Our admiration extends beyond our cover star, as this issue also celebrates the voices of other talented authors who have graced our interviews. We recognize the contributions of Arielle S. Allistarike Kimmel, Jennifer Sommer, Aidan McNally, Alison Ragsdale, CC Robinson, Diana M. Howell, J.R. Rice, Luce Sutherland, Matthew Hughes, Tong Ge, Tyler Beauchamp, Eleanor D. Alspaugh, LB Harpdog, Michael Goddart, Paul J. Jackson, Shari Emami, Sheryl Ickes, Stella Atrium, and Allistar Banks. Each has enriched the literary world with unique stories and perspectives that continue to inspire our readers.

As you explore this issue, may the stories within kindle a newfound appreciation for the wonder and transformative power of literature. We are honoured to share this literary adventure with you and look forward to more stories that not only entertain but also open doors to new worlds and experiences.

Happy reading,
Anna Harlowe

PUBLISHER: READER'S HOUSE MAGAZINE, A Subsidiary of NewYox Media Group. 200 Suite 134-146 Curtain Road, EC2A 3AR London, United Kingdom t: +44 79 3847 8420
editor@readershouse.co.uk II http://readershouse.co.uk II http://newyox.media
EDITORIAL: Anna Harlowe Editor-in-Chief, Dan Peters, Managing Editor, Ben Alan, Art Editor, Z. Robers , Content Editor.
CONTRIBUTORS Claudine D. Reyes, Mickey Mikkelson, Andrea Piacquadio, Adrian T. Cheng, Donna Schim, Jon Allo, Tim Halloran, Oleg Magni, Amir SeilSepour, Bill Youngblood, Jetty Stutzman, Jimmy Choo, Peter Filinovich.

A Thought-Provoking Conversation on Media, Technology, and the Power of Storytelling

Arielle S. Emmett discusses her debut novel The Logoharp, blending science fiction with journalism, exploring disinformation, AI-driven media, and cultural influences that shape narratives in a dystopian yet eerily familiar future.

ARIELLE S. EMMETT

EXPLORES THE FUTURE OF JOURNALISM, AI, AND TRUTH IN THE LOGOHARP

Editor's Desk I London

"The stories we rarely tell, and the ones we encounter accidentally, are those that interest me most."

Arielle S. Emmett is no stranger to the power of storytelling, whether through journalism or fiction. With a distinguished career spanning continents and disciplines, she has reported from East Asia, Africa, and beyond, bringing a sharp analytical lens to global affairs. As a journalist, her work has graced the pages of Smithsonian Air & Space, Mother Jones, The Scientist, and numerous other esteemed publications. Now, with her debut science fiction novel The Logoharp, she ventures into a speculative future where media manipulation, artificial intelligence, and political intrigue intertwine in unsettling ways.

In our conversation, Emmett offers a glimpse into the creative and intellectual forces that shaped The Logoharp. She draws from her deep well of experience—years of investigative journalism, a life lived across cultures, and a profound understanding of shifting global narratives. Her protagonist, Naomi, a journalist-turned-cybernetic media agent, embodies the ethical dilemmas of a world where information is both a tool and a weapon. Emmett's reflections on truth, disinformation, and the evolution of media resonate powerfully in our own era, making her novel not only a gripping tale of the future but also a mirror to the present.

Beyond the novel's thrilling premise, Emmett discusses the intersection of fact and fiction, the challenges of world-building, and the responsibility of writers to engage with complex, cross-cultural themes. Her insights reveal a writer unafraid to wrestle with the big questions—about technology, politics, and the human condition. In this interview, she shares her journey, the inspirations behind The Logoharp, and her thoughts on where science fiction, and perhaps the world itself, might be heading.

What inspired you to blend science fiction with elements of your journalistic background in The Logoharp?

Our global media landscape has changed radically in the last decades, perhaps as much as technological advancements and AI have changed us.

With a few rare exceptions, news organizations no longer act as independent monitors of power; nor do most emphasize meticulous fact checking and presentation of multiple perspectives. Instead virtually all news is channelized according to an agenda, much of it driven by partisan media bosses who build their economic models based on the specific tastes, preferences and values of targeted audiences.

Watching all of this happen during my long career as a science and international journalist, I envisioned a near-future heroine, Naomi, who "writes the future" on behalf of a global power (in this case, China) by seeking "the truth of probable outcomes." In many ways, Naomi is mimicking the way journalists today frame and "predict" the very likely direction of near-term political and social events. Naomi's becomes only half-human, a bio-mechanically enhanced "Reverse Journalist" cyborg reporter for China. She's equipped with a neural instrument, the "Logoharp," which doubles the size of her brain and allows her to speak and broadcast in 104 world languages. She's driven by voices she hears in her AI-infused Logoharp, which filters and directs conversation and instructions from the State, but also from signal sources she can't readily identify. Naomi then "reports the future" to the masses, as though it has already happened—and then it does. Confusion and incredulity result. But eventually the masses come to accept the reality she creates. This, to me, speaks to our media landscape today with its polarizing and often tragic results.

How do you think your extensive travel and experience in diverse cultures have influenced your writing?

I've now lived, reported and taught in Europe, Taiwan, Beijing, Hong Kong, parts of Indonesia, and, more recently, Nairobi, Kenya on a Fulbright Scholarship studying the Chinese presence in East Africa. Obviously just living in these countries, absorbing the literature and close friendships I've made produces insights, contradictions and many questions. I guess I've been encouraged (forced?) to understand cross-cultural perspectives very different from my own. The most jarring differences were encountered in China and Taiwan over many decades. It helped that I learned Mandarin Chinese in college and continued studying throughout my career. But overall, travel in multiple countries helped broaden my awareness of subject matter. The stories we rarely tell, and the ones we encounter accidentally, are those that interest me most. In The Logoharp I tried to incorporate Chinese phrases and terms of art to make Naomi's world more authentic.

> A gripping exploration of media's evolving role, The Logoharp is a bold, insightful, and unsettlingly plausible vision of the future.

Can you share your process for creating the futuristic world in The Logoharp? What was the most challenging aspect?

The futuristic world I built over a period of 12 years (really!) came to me in dreams, shards of autobiography, especially in the early parts of the novel, and, of course, distinct memories of characters I encountered in Taiwan, China and Hong Kong. Naomi, my heroine, was probably the most challenging character of all. The Logoharp's main character, was the most challenging. In this story, she starts as a vulnerable American journalist and morphs into an AI-driven media propagandist for China who eventually rebels. Why would she do this? She lives in a severely weakened "Ameriguo" in the 22nd century. Betrayed by a young lover, she believes that "Mother Country" (China), the dominant global power, will ensure peace and a harmonious existence for a troubled planet—and a glorious career in media for herself. Aside from Naomi, some of the physical transport scenes – specifically the underseas luges enabling Naomi and her lover Marco to cross the Pacific at near hypersonic speeds—came to me from research I did while writing for Smithsonian Air & Space, The Bent, and other magazines. The world I created to describe the ice sleighs (cryo-pods) carrying "the dreaming dead" in Harbin came from actual visits to Manchuria in 2016 during the International Ice Festival. I also recall a short story written by my late mother, Nathalie Donnet, a teacher and excellent theatrical director. In her story she described how our grandparents were "preserved" in glass coffins for all to see. And they were still alive! Her way of suggesting how society treats the elderly. I readily "stole" that idea. So there were many sources to build this world, including articles I wrote on the Chinese space program, especially the lunar missions. In terms of "Life Clocks," Fritz Lang's Metropolis was another inspiration.

How do you navigate the complex themes of disinformation and truth in your work?

I think you have to read The Logoharp to get answers to this question. In some instances I parodied actual news events that were so absurd and horrific that they were funny in the retelling. In other instances I made up stuff based on Chinese, American, and North Korean witchhunts. Naomi's attitudes toward "truth" and even "truthiness" are complex; she's by no means a demonic character; she's trying to do the right thing, and the multiple voices she hears in her Logoharp confuse her at times. Also, her algorithmic evaluation of political scenarios and outcomes always contains some "grain of future truth." She reassures herself that she's broadcasting appropriate reports...until she's not.

Given your experience with both journalism and fiction, how do you balance fact-based writing with imaginative storytelling?

I'm not sure I "balanced" anything. I've always loved fact-based writing, but imaginative storytelling is a whole other skill, aka "altitude of mind." In my case, I had to free up my imagination, to trust it after years of being a "fact head." I had to uncover the emotions and yes, the pain of trying to reconcile what one "should do" given the facts of our society, our identity, our gifts (our lack of fame!) and what one "must do" to honor onself, to make sense of why we're here. I can honestly say that "dreaming the language" of The Logoharp allowed me to write it, to free up the more constrained journalistic sides of my training. I also believe that cinema had a big effect on the structure of the narrative. A lot of readers have told me, "This is a movie!" which surprised me at first. I thought I was writing a novel.

What role do you believe science fiction plays in addressing contemporary political and social issues?

A big role. I don't think most science fiction I read today, especially Chinese science fiction, "wants" or can address contemporary political issues a direct way. Multiple reasons, but one of them is China's criteria for censorship. There are some notable exceptions, of course: Liu Cixin's The Three-Body Problem, an incredible work of imagination, briefly addresses the devastating effects of China's Cultural Revolution. Many other Chinese science fiction writers find solace in ghost stories, solipsism, ancestor worship, sleights of mind, time warps, and of course, alien invasions. In the Western sci-fi world, novels like Octavia Butler's Kindred, for example, or Paolo Bacigalupi's The Windup Girl, Adam Johnson's The Orphan Master's Son, and William Gibson's work have important political and dystopic themes. But I don't know where all of it is heading. I can only imagine a science fiction that addresses both human frailty along with the evolving mastery of technology and AI. What will the intersection of the two bring to our societies of the near future? And how will we foil the villains?

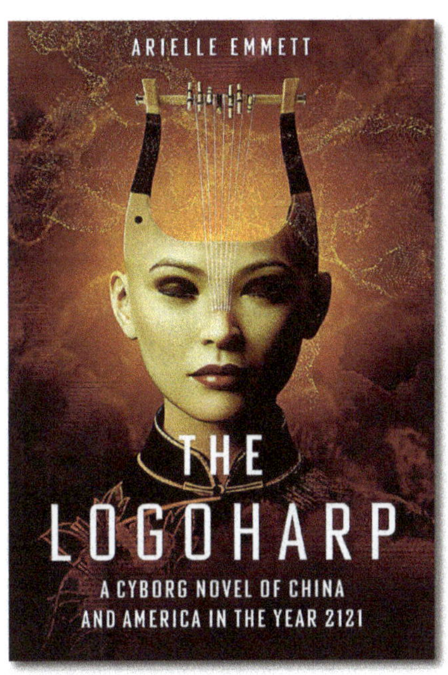

> *The Logoharp* seamlessly blends cyberpunk and profound philosophical inquiry. Arielle Emmett's portrayal of Naomi, a half-cyborg journalist navigating a complex future, is both gripping and thought-provoking. The narrative challenges conventional journalism and examines identity, culture, and morality. A striking and innovative read that lingers long after the last page.

What advice would you give to other writers who are interested in tackling complex, cross-cultural topics in their work?

Spend time in the countries and cultures you write about. Get to know the language and the people. Otherwise, it's "true fakery" or "fake news." The smartest readers will know the difference.

A Journey Through His Creative Process And Impact On Young Actors

In this interview, Mike Kimmel discusses his creative process, impactful educational resources, and the importance of authenticity for young actors.

MIKE KIMMEL

ILLUMINATES THE WORLD OF PERFORMING ARTS WITH PASSION AND INSIGHT

Editot's Desk I London

"Much of the existing material was mean-spirited, snarky, and sarcastic. I felt our younger actors deserved much better than that."

Mike Kimmel stands as a truly multifaceted talent in the performing arts, transcending the boundaries of traditional roles to inspire both audiences and aspiring actors alike. With an impressive background as a former professional wrestler and circus magician, he has masterfully transitioned into the realms of film, television, and theatre, showcasing his versatility and commitment to the craft. His extensive experience has seen him collaborate with some of the industry's most revered directors, while his television credits illuminate his talent across a diverse range of shows, from the likes of *Buffy the Vampire Slayer* to *Game of Silence*.

In addition to his impressive acting career, Kimmel's contributions as a writer and educator are equally commendable. He has penned twelve books that illuminate the challenges and joys of performing arts, cementing his status as a pivotal figure in nurturing the next generation of actors. Works such as *Scenes for Teens* reflect his dedication to providing young performers with meaningful, positive material, demonstrating a keen awareness of the unique emotional landscapes navigated by adolescent actors. His ability to translate complex adult experiences into relatable, engaging dialogues for younger audiences is a testament to his creative genius and pedagogical insight.

As an accomplished educator, Kimmel has inspired countless students, instilling in them not only the skills necessary for success in the performing arts but also a profound appreciation for storytelling and character development. His passion for nurturing talent is evident in his approach, encouraging young actors to explore their authenticity and express their unique voices. It is this blend of experience, creativity, and compassion that has endeared him to both his students and fellow professionals.

In this exclusive interview with Reader's House magazine, Kimmel shares invaluable insights into his creative process, the challenges he has faced, and the wisdom he has gained throughout his illustrious career. Readers will find inspiration in his words, learning about the significance of resilience, authenticity, and the transformative power of theatre in today's digital age. Join us as we delve into the mind of a remarkable artist whose contributions to the performing arts continue to resonate, enrich, and inspire.

What inspired you to write "Scenes for Teens" and how do you feel it has impacted young actors?

"Scenes for Teens" was my first book and grew out of my classes for child and teenage actors. I previously taught acting classes for adults and was very experienced in that area. I had hundreds of great scripts to draw upon—from years of auditions and paid acting work in New York and Los Angeles. When I started preparing to teach my new classes for younger actors, unfortunately, I found that there was a real lack of quality scripts available for kids, tweens, and teens. Much of the existing material was mean-spirited, snarky, and sarcastic. I felt our younger actors deserved much better than that. I started writing two-character dialogues for my classes—and decided to embed positive messages, optimistic ideas, and philosophical life lessons into the scenes as subtext.

While testing these teenage scenes in class, I also started writing scenes for younger actors, aged six to twelve. Those dialogues eventually became my second book, "Acting Scenes for Kids and Tweens." We all need positive messages these days, and young actors probably need them most of all. The sensitivity and emotional vulnerability that makes someone (of any age) a good actor often makes it difficult to navigate the harsh realities of the entertainment industry—the competitiveness, uncertainty, and frequent rejection.

Can you describe your creative process when developing monologues for kids and tweens?

I like to look at our world—and especially at situations I'm dealing with as an adult—and try to imagine those exact same scenarios through the eyes of a much younger person who hasn't yet developed the maturity, social skills, and real-life experience to handle them. Then I like to write scenes and monologues about our adult world from the point of view of that younger person. For example, a few years back, a man ran out of his house and started screaming at me because I parked (in a legal parking spot) in front of his house. He was an elderly man and I was pretty shocked at his childish behavior.

> Mike Kimmel is a brilliant educator and storyteller, whose dedication to nurturing young talent transforms the landscape of performing arts.

Instead of becoming angry, though, I asked myself, "How can I use this?" This is a question I also ask myself as an actor. (It's a wonderful technique, in fact, for handling many challenging situations in our daily lives.) I was writing my fourth book, "Monologues for Kids and Tweens" at the time, and decided to use this screaming man as the subject of a monologue for younger kids. Imagine being an eight year old living across the street from this angry man and watching him go berserk on anyone who dared park in front of his house. Imagine being a kid whose parents tell him to respect his elders—and then seeing this rude, angry man across the street behave so badly again and again. If this incident was awkward for me, I thought, imagine how uncomfortable it would be for an eight year old child. That incident became one of my favorite monologues in the book—and grew out of asking myself the question, "How can I use this?"

What challenges did you face while writing "Six Critical Essays on Film," and how did you overcome them?

Writing "Six Critical Essays on Film" presented a unique challenge for me—which I eagerly embraced. This book was a complete departure from the type of books (and scripts) I usually write, which are primarily dialogue-driven. For years, I pursued a dual career in Education and the Performing Arts. As an educator, I taught classes in Acting, Film and Television History, and Public Speaking in Colleges and Adult Schools. Many of my college students would enroll in a History of Film course to fulfill distribution requirements for graduation. They were looking for a course in the Arts that would be interesting to them and, in most cases, not terribly difficult or demanding. Their reasoning was sound. Everybody likes movies, right? Unfortunately, many students—particularly those with backgrounds in engineering and the hard sciences—had difficulty writing essays about movies. Although they knew what they liked, it was difficult for them to explain why they liked it in an essay.

I wrote this book to help college students break films down into their component parts and evaluate their relative strengths and weaknesses. In this book, I suggested six different areas through which films can be critiqued: storyline and script, directing and editing, acting, lighting and movement, and overall theme, message or ideology.

I also suggested creative thinking strategies to get the attention of their college professors. Imagine alternate endings for the films we study in class. Imagine actors from another generation playing the leads in our favorite films. Imagine Scarlett Johansson going back in time to 1946 and playing Rita Hayworth's role in "Gilda." Imagine Humphrey Bogart and Clark Gable leaping forward in time to play the George Clooney and Brad Pitt roles in "Oceans Eleven." These are outside-the-box ideas that can really capture a professor's attention.

In your opinion, what are the most important skills a young actor should develop?

Young actors need to learn to make strong choices with scripts—and use their imaginations to create rich, full back-stories to the characters they're playing. One way to develop this skill is to ask yourself: "What was I doing right before the action in the scene I'm playing interrupted me?" For example, if you have a tiny role in a play or a movie and you're just walking onto an elevator and saying "Good morning" to the lead actor, your character still has a history, an outside life, and a unique viewpoint about the world. Your character didn't just pop into existence at the precise moment you walked into the elevator. Something was happening in that character's life. Something was going on before that elevator door opened. If you can figure out how to convey that character's inner life—within the context of the script and without distracting attention from the lead players—you will connect very well with audiences. Audiences will always pick up on that authenticity.

How do you see the role of theatre and performance evolving in today's digital age?

Nothing beats the thrill of performing in live theatre and I believe there is no better training ground for actors. Performing on stage helps actors learn the value of teamwork and understand how the individual efforts of each actor contribute to the overall success of the play. These are skills that translate beautifully into television and film. Working on stage teaches actors stagecraft, voice control and modulation, comedic timing, and how to think quickly on their feet. Theatre actors learn to figure out what to do when props aren't working or a cast member misses an important cue. They learn how to make adjustments—and get the storyline back on track— when a fellow actor skips a line of dialogue. They learn not to get rattled when the audience doesn't respond as expected.

There will always be advancements in technology. That has been true ever since the early days of silent film. No matter what the future brings, however, I believe that actors with solid theatre experience in front of live audiences will always be at a significant advantage over their non-theatre trained colleagues.

What advice would you give to aspiring authors looking to create impactful educational resources in the performing arts?

Remember not to talk down to our young people—and to adult actors who are new to the business. Just because someone is new to the entertainment industry doesn't mean they have nothing to offer. I love working with talented young people. I get inspired and motivated by their energy and enthusiasm. Every actor has talent that can be developed, and every writer has a story to share with the world. Experienced actors and writers need to build up the next generation of performing artists in our industry—or we'll have no industry fifty years from now. It ends with us.

I also think everyone has a book inside them that is literally screaming for an opportunity to be revealed and "birthed out" into the world. Not every writer can become a number one bestselling author, of course, but everyone has a unique point of view and a significant set of skills to share. There are no boring people out there—only people who have not yet found their niche and their unique, authentic voice (or are purposely hiding their true talents and desires from themselves and the world). If you ever find yourself bored or simply disinterested when talking with someone, it's because you're not digging deep enough. Everyone has a story to share; some people just need a little extra help finding it.

The best way to find your authentic voice is to diligently sit down at your writing table every day and get to work. Sweat it out. Put it all down on paper. Some of it may not be any good, but through the process of writing the bad work you will ultimately find the good work. Writing every day will help you figure out what you believe in—and who you really are as an artist.

I once told a writer friend who was struggling in this area: "You don't have the right to keep your gifts and talents from the world." That's now become a favorite catchphrase between me and my closest friends. We may envy the skill set of a colleague from time to time, but always remember that someone in this world needs what you have to offer. We don't gain much in life from holding back, and the world gains nothing when we keep our gifts and talents hidden—and our best stories locked away in a bottom desk drawer.

Her Journey From Librarian to Literary Success

Jennifer Sommer discusses her transition from children's librarian to acclaimed author, sharing insights about her award-winning books, research process, and dedication to inspiring young readers.

JENNIFER SOMMER

A STELLAR RISE IN CHILDREN'S LITERATURE FROM LIBRARY DESK TO BESTSELLER LISTS CREATING MAGIC FOR YOUNG MINDS

"Any time a book wins an award, it boosts my confidence a little bit more, because this business is so full of rejection."

by Dan Peters I London

Jennifer Sommer, the remarkable American author whose literary prowess has captivated young readers across the globe, graces the pages of our magazine this month. Her stellar achievements, including the prestigious Kirkus Star and recognition in the Best of Indie Books 2024, showcase her exceptional talent in children's literature.

The Kentucky-born author's journey from children's librarian to acclaimed writer is nothing short of inspiring. Her latest works, *Her Eyes Were On The Stars (2023)* and *Every Creature Eats* (2024), have established her as a formidable voice in children's literature. The former, a masterful biography of Nancy Grace Roman, has earned widespread acclaim, whilst the latter delights young readers with its clever blend of humour and culinary adventure.

As Editor of Reader's House, I am particularly thrilled to present this intimate conversation with Sommer, whose academic achievements - spanning political science, interior design, architecture, and library science - reflect her boundless intellectual curiosity. Her transition from beloved children's librarian to award-winning author exemplifies the power of pursuing one's dreams, regardless of timing.

In this exclusive interview, Sommer shares fascinating insights into her creative process, research methodology, and the inspiration behind her compelling works. She also discusses her upcoming projects, including *The Changeling* and *Octopus Capers*, both currently with the esteemed Jennifer De Chiara Literary Agency.

We are honoured to bring you this candid conversation with one of contemporary children's literature's most engaging voices. Her story is not just about writing books; it's about inspiring the next generation of readers and dreamers.

What inspired you to write 'Her Eyes Were on the Stars', and how did you approach researching Nancy Grace Roman's life?

My inspiration came from a show about the Hubble telescope when Nancy Grace Roman was mentioned as "the Mother of Hubble". I had never heard of her. I wasn't sure if she was still living, but found her email listed on the NASA website. My approach was as easy as emailing her and asking for a telephone interview. Our second interview was in person near Washington D.C. She was 91 years old at the time. Luckily, I recorded both interviews, because her actual quotes ended up being an important part of my final manuscript. That was the beginning.

Sommer's masterful storytelling and dedication to children's literature have earned her well-deserved recognition and inspired countless young minds.

Could you share the process behind creating *'Every Creature Eats'* and how your experience as a children's librarian influenced its development?

I worked as a Children's Librarian for nearly 20 years, mainly with school aged kids, ages 6-12. One of my favorite programs was an annual Mad Scientists Lab my department created as an alternative to a Halloween Party. We wanted to infuse an educational element while also making it fun. We dressed up as mad scientists in our lab coats and safety glasses, and spent the first part of the program performing science experiments. Then we served snacks to go along with the theme. Another after school program I held was the Gross Grub Club where I read chapters from an appropriately gross book to the kids each week and we enjoyed gross snacks. So, 'Every Creature Eats' grew from my desire to create that kind of experience for young children. In this case, a witch is having a party and serving all these disgusting-sounding treats that are actually very yummy.

How did your background in children's literature and your MFA in creative writing shape your writing style and choice of subjects?

We were encouraged to try different genres during the MFA program, but I always leaned towards writing non-fiction. Non-fiction books for children are so informative. In our children's department at the library, we wrote book reviews and I gravitated toward writing those for non-fiction books, especially science subjects. I even served on the American Library Association's (ALA) Sibert committee that chose the best non-fiction books for children in 2016. So, I've read lots of non-fiction, and was very aware of the current market as well as the kinds of things that would be useful in our library. I love research, and as a librarian, I can research the heck out of anything. It's a good fit for me. I have also written fantasy and historical fiction, which also require some research. Poetry, though, isn't in my wheelhouse. 'Every Creature Eats' is probably the most rhyming you'll see from me!

What challenges did you face when transitioning from a children's librarian to a full-time author, and how did you overcome them?

One of the biggest concerns was going from a very structured schedule to having none. I knew I could easily let everything slide if I didn't set up at least a bit of structure, so I prepared a home office, but found that I wasn't always very productive working there. Writing at the library every day worked out much better. Joining three different critique groups kept me accountable. I joined SCBWI (Society of Children's Book Writers and Illustrators) and attended monthly meetings, as well as regional workshops in person and online to keep learning. I also volunteered on ALA committees to keep current on literature for kids. Still, I don't work full-time by any means.

How did winning the Karen and Philip Cushman Late Bloomer Award impact your writing career and confidence as an author?

It validated my decision to try and realize my childhood dream of writing. It proved to me that I could write, and write about something that would interest someone else. The manuscript that won that award is 'Octopus Capers', a non-fiction picture book about octopuses and their behavior. It's currently with my agent, Stephen Fraser of Jennifer De Chiara Literary Agency. Any time a book wins an award, it boosts my confidence a little bit more, because this business is so full of rejection.

Can you discuss the significance of the Kirkus Star and being included in the Best of Indie Books 2024 for 'Her Eyes Were on the Stars'?

What an honor! KIRKUS Magazine reviews thousands of books and gives a star to a small percentage of books considered to have exceptional merit. Libraries around the country use KIRKUS as a way to determine which books to purchase for their library. I had submitted 'Her Eyes Were on the Stars' for a review, and it came back glowing! It was some days before I even realized there was a star attached. The icing on the cake was when the e-mail came saying my book would be included on the Best of Indie Books 2024 list. I had to keep it a secret for several months until the article was published, which was excruciating for me because I wanted to tell everyone!

This book chronicles Nancy Grace Roman's journey from astronomy enthusiast to NASA's first female executive. Jennifer Sommer's accessible writing and Sophia Kia's narration effectively portray Roman's challenges and achievements, particularly her role in creating the Hubble Space Telescope, though some parts feel rushed.

What are some of the most rewarding experiences you've had during author visits and presentations, particularly those related to your books?

Probably my favorite event was one at a local observatory. I read 'Her Eyes Were on the Stars' to the group, which describes how astronomers wanted a telescope in space due to the effects of the earth's atmosphere which distorts what we see. There was a simple demonstration representing the effect and then the group could view stars through three different telescopes. I love this type of event that really expands on the book. Plus, I had a few kids show up to get a book signed by a real, live, author!

What advice would you offer to aspiring authors looking to write for children and young adults, based on your journey and experiences?

I always encourage joining SCBWI and attending workshops to learn the basics of writing for these groups. There are lots of ins and outs, and trends that come and go. Also, critique groups are invaluable for immediate feedback. It might take trying out a group or two until you find a good fit. I've met great friends and writers through those groups and workshops, and now my middle grade group has started to have getaways at my lake house in Kentucky for some intensive writing and critique time, which I also recommend.

Celebrating The Journey Of A Remarkable Author Dedicated To Enchanting Children's Literature

A.M. BERKOWITZ

INSPIRING YOUNG MINDS THROUGH WHIMSY AND WONDER

AS TOLD TO ZOSIA ROBERTS

A.M. Berkowitz shares her inspiring journey from opera to children's literature, highlighting her passion for fostering joy and creativity in young readers.

A.M. Berkowitz captivates the hearts of young readers with her enchanting stories, making her a standout voice in children's literature. Her delightful works, including the charming debut "Ladybug Kisses – Besos De Mariquita" and the beloved "Gigglet the Happy Little Piglet" series, have garnered numerous accolades, spotlighting her remarkable ability to weave joy and imagination into every page. With a unique trajectory that encompasses both an operatic stage background and extensive corporate experience, Berkowitz's journey exemplifies the inspiring truth that it is never too late to follow one's passion and make a profound impact on the lives of others.

Reader's House magazine proudly features A.M. Berkowitz on our cover this month, celebrating her significant contributions to children's literature and her heartfelt mission to inspire creativity and joy among young readers. Her stories bring laughter, warmth, and invaluable life lessons, encouraging children to embrace the wonder of reading and discover their own imaginations. Through her engaging narratives, Berkowitz not only entertains but also fosters emotional resilience, equipping young minds with the tools they need to navigate their world with positivity and empathy.

In our exclusive star interview, readers will gain insight into Berkowitz's creative process, her motivations for establishing AMB Kids Books, and her vision for the future of children's literature. Her commitment to creating relatable characters and engaging stories reflects her understanding of the important role that reading plays in a child's development. Moreover, her passion for storytelling goes beyond mere entertainment; it is a heartfelt endeavour aimed at sparking joy and inspiring a lifelong love for literature.

As Berkowitz embarks on new adventures with her beloved characters, including the upcoming tale of Gigglet preparing to welcome a new sibling, her dedication to enriching the reading experience continues to shine through. Join us as we delve into the magical

Continued *on page 20*

"Berkowitz, Author, storyteller, and champion of children's literature, inspiring young hearts and minds through her delightful tales.

Continued *from page 18*

Sparking Smiles: How Berkowitz's Stories Empower Young Minds

A.M. Berkowitz shines as a beacon of creativity and heart, enchanting the world of children's literature with her magical tales and inspiring journey. An award-winning author with a vibrant background—from operatic stages to the corridors of corporate life—Berkowitz's transition into writing has gifted us stories that are as delightful as they are transformative. Her celebrated works, including the charming debut "Ladybug Kisses – Besos De Mariquita" and the ever-beloved "Gigglet the Happy Little Piglet" series, continue to spark joy and nurture imagination among young readers.

world of A.M. Berkowitz and discover how her writing not only entertains but also empowers children and families alike. Celebrating her innovative spirit and genuine love for storytelling, our cover feature is a tribute to an author who is truly making a difference in the literary landscape.

> *"Every story is an adventure waiting to unfold—thank you, A.M. Berkowitz, for filling our world with laughter, love, and learning!"*

Why did you decide to become a writer?

While there isn't just one moment that reaffirms my choice to be a writer, it's really all those little moments that come together to create a beautiful tapestry of joy. Every time I hand a book to a child and see their eyes light up, it fills me with warmth. I love hearing from parents and teachers about how much their kids adore the Gigglet books. It's heartwarming to know that some children take their books with them everywhere they go.

Those moments remind me why I write. Knowing that I've brought a bit of happiness and joy into someone's life is an incredible feeling. It's all about spreading love and kindness through storytelling, and that's what keeps me inspired every day!

What inspired you to establish your company AMB Kids Books, and when did you begin the company?

I'm so glad you asked! The inspiration behind establishing AMB Kids Books came from a deep love for storytelling and a desire to foster a lifelong passion for reading in children. I noticed how powerful stories can be in sparking imagination and creativity, and I wanted to create a space where kids could explore diverse narratives and characters.

I officially started the company in January 2024, aiming to provide engaging, relatable, and educational content that resonates with young readers, teachers, parents and guardians. It's been a wonderful journey so far, and I'm excited to keep creating books that inspire and entertain!

Could you tell me more about the types of children's books you specialize in?

Absolutely! I personally love picture books/board books. I enjoy reading these books more than adult books. These books are perfect for the youngest readers, typically (ages 0-5). They combine beautiful illustrations with simple, engaging stories that help spark imagination and language development. My books are geared toward early readers: Aimed at children who are just starting to read on their own (ages 4-6), these books feature larger text, shorter sentences, repetitive words, and include bright and colorful illustrations that support comprehension.

Do your books focus on any specific themes, genres, or age groups?

My books focus on themes of happiness, joy and wonderment. These emotions are fundamental to a child's development and understanding of the world around them. When kids encounter stories that emphasize joy, they learn to recognize and appreciate positive feelings, which can help shape their emotional resilience.

Joyful narratives can spark imagination and creativity, encouraging children to explore their own emotions and experiences. Happiness also fosters connection—stories filled with joy can help children relate to others and develop empathy. Ultimately, by highlighting happiness and joy, these books aim to create a sense of wonder and positivity, enriching the reading experience and supporting emotional growth. After all, who doesn't love a good tale that leaves them smiling?

Are your books available in both print

and digital formats, and where can readers purchase them?

Yes! Absolutely! I'm thrilled to share that my books are available in both print and digital formats. You can easily find them on Amazon.com through my author central site at Amazon Author where they're flying off the shelves! If you happen to find them sold out, don't hesitate to reach out - just email me at ambkids-books@gmail.com and I'll be happy to help you get a copy.

Plus, I'm excited to announce that you'll soon be able to purchase my books directly through my new online store at www.ambkidsbooks.com. Stay tuned for updates, and thank you for your support! Happy Reading!

Do you create any interactive or educational resources to accompany your books?

Yes! As a matter of fact I do! "Gigglet The Happy Little Piglet" series comes with a variety of interactive and educational resources to enrich the reading experience. Each of the three charming board books has its own companion activity/coloring book designed specifically for early readers.

But that's not all! My website is packed with fun interactive features, including a digital memory game that kids can enjoy, a comprehensive Printables section where you can find coloring pages and activity sheets to download and print, and even a delightful area filled with Gigglet-themed recipes to try out together.

And here's a little sneak peek: Gigglet is now available as a lovable, huggable, squeezable plush toy! This adorable little piglet will be available for purchase in my upcoming online store, making story time even more special. With Gigglet by their side, young readers can dive into the magic of the stories while cuddling their new piggy friend. Stay tuned for the launch—I can't wait to share Gigglet with all of you!

Do you have plans to release any new titles or series in the near future?

Oh my goodness! Yes! I have some exciting new titles and series on the horizon! Our beloved Gigglet is about to embark on a heartwarming adventure as she prepares to become a big sister! This upcoming story will beautifully capture the joy and emotions of welcoming a new baby brother into the family. It's a tale that promises to resonate with young readers and fill their hearts with warmth.

AND! There are more enchanting stories and characters joining the lineup! We can't wait to share these delightful adventures with you and your little ones. Stay tuned for all the fun and giggles coming your way!

What is your primary aim or mission when producing books for young readers?

My primary aim when creating books for young readers is to inspire a love for reading and learning. I want to create stories that spark imagination and curiosity, encouraging kids to explore new ideas and perspectives. It's important to me that these books are not only engaging but also age-appropriate, featuring relatable characters and themes that resonate with young readers.

I strive to foster wonderment, creativity, and critical thinking through diverse narratives, ensuring that children see themselves reflected in the stories they read. Ultimately, my mission is to make

Continued *on page 22*

Continued *from page 21*

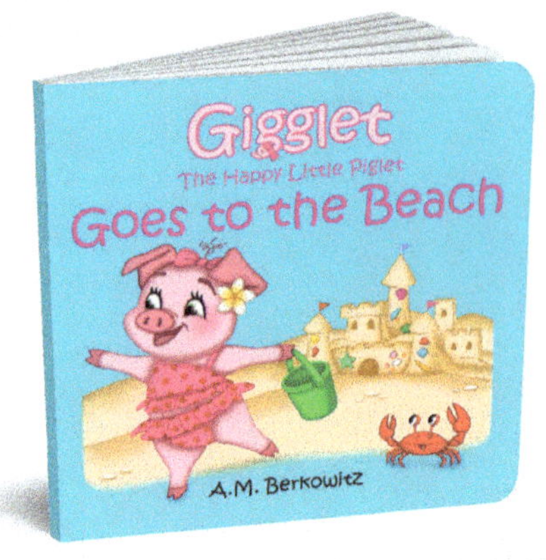

reading a joyful and enriching experience, laying the foundation for lifelong learning and a deeper understanding of the world around them.

What are the key messages or lessons children can learn from your books?

Every day, children are presented with countless choices that shape their experiences and emotions. I want them to understand that they have the ability to choose how they feel, no matter what circumstances they face.

Life is a colorful mix of emotions, and while we can't control everything that happens, we can control our responses. By consciously choosing uplifting thoughts and embracing happiness, children can develop a positive mindset that not only enhances their own well-being but also spreads joy to those around them.

Wouldn't it be something if children grew up knowing they have the power to navigate life's challenges with resilience! By embracing this truth, they can face obstacles with optimism, gratitude, and a belief that they truly can shape their experiences. It's all about empowering them to recognize that their thoughts and feelings are within their control. With this understanding, they can thrive and create a ripple effect of positivity that touches everyone they meet!

If you could talk to your younger self at the beginning of your writing journey, what would you say?

"Amber! You have so much potential—remember the journey is just as important as the destination. Embrace the ups and downs; every experience shapes you as a writer and creator. Trust your inner voice. It's okay to stumble; keep going and creating. Find joy in the little things, allow those happy thoughts to flow, and don't forget to 'Get Your Giggle On'—laughter fuels creativity. Life is an adventure, and writing is a beautiful part of it. Relish every moment and every story. You're meant to shine, and I can't wait to see you light up the world!"

Summer Adventures with Gigglet: A Whimsical Journey for Young Readers

A.M. Berkowitz's "*Gigglet The Happy Little Piglet*" series is a heartwarming and enchanting collection of children's books, delivering delightful tales that inspire joy, wonder, and appreciation for life's simple pleasures. From going to summer camp to splashing at the beach, these books invite young readers to immerse themselves in Gigglet's adventures, encouraging playful imagination and an emotional connection with her world.

A.M. Berkowitz's delightful books charm children with heartwarming stories, vibrant illustrations, and joyful adventures that spark imagination and laughter!

Gigglet The Happy Little Piglet Goes to Summer Camp, available as both a board book and Kindle Edition, is a stellar masterpiece. The vibrant illustrations by Nifty Illustration bring to life the essence of summer camp with remarkable charm. Berkowitz's storytelling creates a captivating narrative of fun-filled activities like canoeing, gift-making, and outdoor games while emphasizing nature's beauty and childhood camaraderie. This book, rated 4.7 stars for the board format and an impressive 5.0 stars for the Kindle Edition, successfully engages readers with its warmth and life lessons. It's a perfect choice for summer reading and a treasure for families seeking to share meaningful moments.

Gigglet The Happy Little Piglet Goes to the Beach, brings summertime magic with its cheerful narrative and lively scenes of beachside antics. Berkowitz, with her unique charm, crafts Gigglet's beach-day adventure in a way that will make young readers and parents smile, laugh, and appreciate the carefree spirit of childhood. Accompanied by Nifty Illustration's beautiful artwork, the story draws readers into a jubilant world of sun, sand, and giggles.

A.M. Berkowitz's books celebrate the joy of childhood, friendship, and the beauty of nature, making them invaluable additions to any child's bookshelf. Whether visiting the beach or camp through Gigglet's eyes, these stories leave behind cherished memories, fostering imagination and a love for adventure in the hearts of children worldwide.

FROM SMALL TOWN TO LITERARY STARDOM

The Inspiring Journey of
ALLISTAR BANKS

Allistar Banks shares her journey from a small-town upbringing to becoming a celebrated author, discussing her inspirations, community involvement, and the impact of her books on readers of all ages.

Allistar Banks is a shining example of how passion and perseverance can transform dreams into reality. Hailing from the charming town of McCormick, South Carolina, Allistar's journey from a small-town girl to a renowned author and community leader is a testament to her unwavering dedication and talent. Her early career as a news reporter honed her storytelling skills, allowing her to craft narratives that captivate and inspire readers of all ages. With two published books, "Nosy Nicole and the Red Airplane" and "A Journey Unfolds," Allistar has established herself as a beloved author in both children's and adult fiction. Her stories are not only entertaining but also resonate deeply with readers, offering valuable life lessons and insights.

Allistar's contributions extend beyond her literary achievements. As a dedicated member of the Augusta Women's Club and the Community Service Project leader on the Board of Education, she exemplifies the spirit of giving back to the community that shaped her. Her commitment to education and community service reflects her deep-rooted values and her desire to make a positive impact. Allistar Banks is a true inspiration, and her story is a powerful reminder of the endless possibilities that await those who dare to pursue their passions.

Lenny the Lizard and His Green Scarf and A Colorful Balloon Ride both focus on important lessons for young readers. What inspired you to create stories that emphasize themes like sharing and learning through adventure?

Lenny the Lizard and His Green Scarf and A Colorful Balloon Ride both focus on important lessons for young readers. What inspired you to create stories that emphasize themes like sharing and learning through adventure? I was inspired to write Lenny the Lizard and His Green Scarf because I grew up around my families farm in South Carolina and I noticed how happy and joyful a little green lizard was one day and he seemed to make the other farm animals feel happy that were a pig, a random mouse running around, and I loved otters from going on a trip to the South Carolina Aquarium as a second grade student and decided to tie an otter into the story. I received a green scarf and cashmere sweater growing up that helped me to feel good when I felt down and out. A Colorful Balloon Ride was inspired off of how I learned colors in my kindergarten art class with my best friend Emily and I loved going to the County Fair growing up.

Growing up in McCormick, South Carolina, and later studying Mass Communications, how have your roots and educational background influenced your writing style and the themes you choose to explore in your books?

Growing up in McCormick, South Carolina, and later studying Mass Communications, how have your roots and educational background influenced your writing style and the themes you choose to explore in your books?

Growing up in McCormick, South Carolina and my degree in Mass Communications have influenced my writing style by growing up in the south and being influenced by southern culture while learning the professional writing style of drafting interviews and stories that were local and national.

Spring Brings Summer" by Allistar Banks beautifully captures the essence of seasonal change, offering readers a delightful journey through nature's transformations with vivid imagery and heartwarming storytelling that enchants both children and adults.

Your books have been featured in various publications and media outlets. How has this exposure impacted your journey as an author, and what does it mean to you to see your work recognized in your community and beyond?

Your books have been featured in various publications and media outlets. How has this exposure impacted your journey as an author, and what does it mean to you to see your work recognized in your community and beyond?

It has gained new followers to follow my stories and work and wanting more content. It means a lot to me because I have always wanted my writing to be known all around the world because writing gives me a time and space to express my creativity and what brings me true joy in life.

Children's literature often serves as a tool for teaching life lessons. How do you approach writing stories that are not only engaging for children but also convey meaningful messages that resonate with both kids and adults?

Children's literature often serves as a tool for teaching life lessons. How do you approach writing stories that are not only engaging for children but also convey meaningful messages that resonate with both kids and adults?

I approach writing for children and adults by exploring how both children and adults can make a connection with one another and what both have in common.

As an author with a background in Mass Communications, how do you leverage your communication skills to connect with your audience and promote your work effectively?

As an author with a background in Mass Communications, how do you leverage your communication skills to connect with your audience and promote your work effectively?

I leverage my communication skills by actively listening and understanding non-verbal cues. Active listening is essential for effective communication. I also exude confidence and adapt the message to my target audience.

What advice would you give to aspiring authors who are just starting their journey, especially those who want to write stories for children that are both entertaining and educational?

What advice would you give to aspiring authors who are just starting their journey, especially those who want to write stories for children that are both entertaining and educational?

I would research children's books within the particular niche they want to write for through libraries and online.

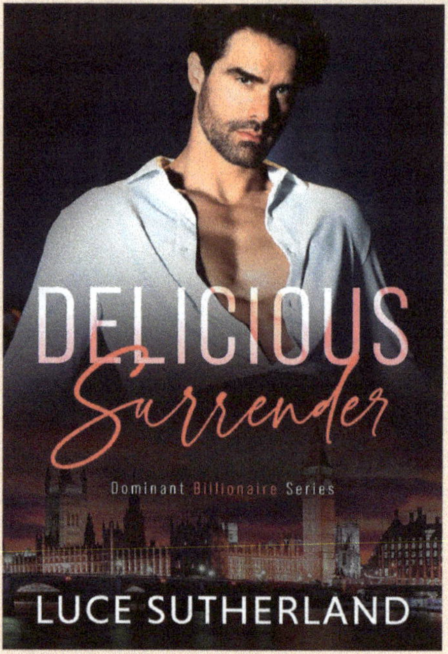

CAGED

by CC Robinson

A gripping, fast-paced dystopian sequel with high stakes, compelling characters, and relentless tension—Caged keeps readers hooked from start to finish.

Caged, the second instalment in CC Robinson's *Divided* series, is a gripping YA dystopian novel that keeps readers on edge from start to finish. Picking up where *Divided* left off, we find protagonist Rose in an even more dire situation—stripped of her freedom, trapped in a literal prison, and cut off from those who once stood by her side.

Robinson crafts a tense, claustrophobic atmosphere that mirrors Rose's predicament, making every chapter pulse with urgency. The stakes are higher than ever, as Rose not only fights for her own survival but also for the future of her city. Her journey from helpless captive to determined fighter is compelling, showcasing resilience and the power of hope in the face of tyranny.

One of the novel's greatest strengths is its pacing. The action never falters, and as Rose unravels the sinister schemes of her captors, the tension builds masterfully. The story is interwoven with moments of reflection and character growth, ensuring that it's not just about high-stakes action but also about the emotional depth of its heroine.

Readers who enjoyed *Divergent or The Giver* will appreciate the familiar dystopian themes, yet *Caged* maintains its own unique identity. With a well-developed world, gripping suspense, and a protagonist worth rooting for, this sequel solidifies the *Divided* series as a must-read for fans of the genre.

An electrifying read that delivers both heart and adrenaline—Robinson does not disappoint.

DELİCIOUS SURRENDER

by Luce Sutherland

Intensely passionate, thrillingly suspenseful, and irresistibly steamy—Delicious Surrender delivers fiery chemistry, gripping tension, and a deeply satisfying romance.

Luce Sutherland delivers a steamy, high-stakes romance in *Delicious Surrender*, the first instalment of the *Dominant Billionaire Series*. With a tantalising mix of power play, sizzling chemistry, and emotional depth, this novel is an enticing read for fans of the grumpy-sunshine trope.

Brynne Larimore, an independent and headstrong writer, finds herself entangled in the dark allure of Club Dominus, a world ruled by the icy and domineering Gage MacLeod. Their dynamic is electric—Brynne's defiance sparks fire against Gage's relentless control, making for an intoxicating push-and-pull. The tension is palpable, with Sutherland masterfully balancing fiery exchanges with moments of raw vulnerability.

While the romance is undeniably steamy, what sets this book apart is its suspenseful undercurrent. The presence of a dangerous Russian club member adds an element of intrigue, forcing Gage to confront not only his protective instincts but also his own vulnerabilities. The stakes rise when betrayal threatens his business, pushing both characters to their limits.

Sutherland's writing is crisp and immersive, painting a vivid picture of London's elite club scene while delving into themes of trust, power, and emotional surrender. The pacing is tight, keeping the reader hooked through every twist and turn.

If you enjoy passionate, angst-ridden romances with dominant yet redeemable heroes, *Delicious Surrender* will not disappoint. The hard-fought happy ending is well-earned, making this a satisfying start to what promises to be a compelling series.

HENCHMEN

by Matthew Hughes

A gripping, witty fantasy adventure with rich world-building, engaging characters, and masterful storytelling—Hughes delivers intrigue, action, and unforgettable magic.

Matthew Hughes' *Henchmen* is a gripping fantasy novel that blends adventure, intrigue, and a touch of dry humour into a thoroughly enjoyable read. Set in a world where even employment is dictated by a Duke's decree, the story follows Vunt, a gambler, and Oldo, a farm boy, as they stumble into a job that is both lucrative and deeply suspicious. Their new employer's shifty dealings soon propel them into a far greater and more dangerous world than they ever imagined.

The novel masterfully balances classic fantasy elements with a refreshing, character-driven narrative. Hughes excels in crafting protagonists who feel authentic—Vunt's cunning contrasts nicely with Oldo's naivety, making their dynamic both engaging and entertaining. As the pair are drawn into a web of espionage, wizardly schemes, and perilous travels, the plot unfolds with a steady momentum that keeps the pages turning.

Hughes' writing is rich yet accessible, reminiscent of classic adventure fantasy but with a modern wit that makes it stand out. The setting is immersive, with detailed world-building that never overwhelms the reader. The city of Olliphract, with its unpredictable thaumaturges, is a particularly fascinating backdrop.

For fans of fantasy that doesn't take itself too seriously yet delivers on action and intrigue, *Henchmen* is a must-read. Hughes proves once again that he is a master of weaving intelligent, well-paced storytelling with a unique voice. Highly recommended.

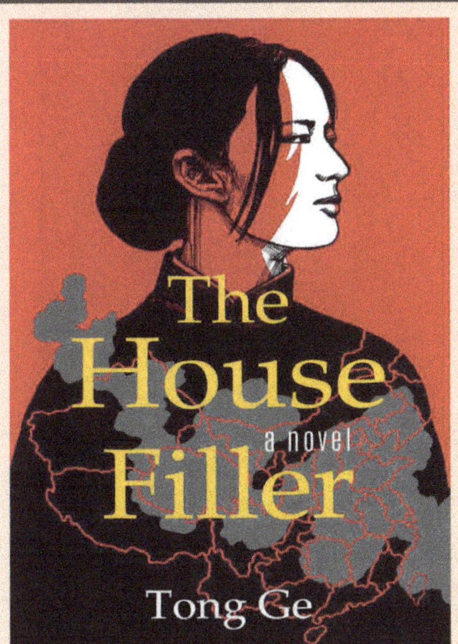

THE HOUSE FİLLER

by Tong Ge

A beautifully written, emotionally powerful novel that captures resilience, love, and survival amidst the turmoil of war and political unrest.

The House Filler is a deeply moving and richly layered novel that captures the personal cost of war and political upheaval through the eyes of a resilient woman, Golden Phoenix. Set against the backdrop of China's civil war and Japanese occupation, Tong Ge's narrative is both heart-wrenching and inspiring.

Golden Phoenix is a formidable protagonist. Following her husband's premature death, she is left to raise her children amidst chaos and uncertainty. Her struggle to preserve her family through famine, violence, and separation forms the emotional core of the novel. The most harrowing moments come during the Japanese occupation, where she and her adopted son face unimaginable suffering. Yet, through it all, her spirit never truly breaks.

Ge's prose is elegant and evocative, immersing the reader in both the beauty and brutality of 20th-century China. The historical detail is meticulously researched, giving the story a powerful sense of authenticity without ever feeling like a history lesson. Characters are vividly drawn, especially the twin daughters and the son who joins the Nationalist army, each of whom adds depth to the family's fractured portrait.

Ending in 1965, on the eve of the Cultural Revolution, the novel leaves readers with a haunting sense of what is still to come. *The House Filler* is not just a tale of survival—it's a tribute to maternal love, endurance, and the quiet strength required to hold a family together in the darkest of times.

Highly recommended for fans of historical fiction with emotional depth.

FROM GREEN TO BLUE

by Jonathan Cox

Authentic, witty, and deeply human—Cox delivers a masterclass in storytelling that captures the heart and grit of real policing.

Jonathan Cox's *From Green to Blue* is a gripping and candid dive into the world of policing, told with the kind of authenticity only a seasoned officer could offer. As the first instalment in *The Nostrils Series*, it introduces readers to Chris Pritchard, a lonely 18-year-old orphan who stumbles into the Metropolitan Police seeking structure, companionship, and a sense of belonging.

Set in London's gritty East End, the novel strikes a fine balance between dark humour and emotional depth. Chris's experiences, shadowed by the sharp-tongued yet oddly nurturing WPC Dawn Matthews, unfold in a series of poignant, often hilarious, and occasionally absurd episodes. Each chapter offers a glimpse into the harsh realities of policing, from violent confrontations to touching human moments, all portrayed without sensationalism.

Cox writes with clarity, wit and emotional intelligence, inviting readers into the camaraderie and chaos of police life in a bygone era. The tone is refreshingly unpretentious, capturing both the mundanity and madness of life on the beat. What makes this book particularly compelling is its quiet honesty—there's no glamorisation, only gritty truths softened with sharp observational humour.

With over 5,000 glowing reviews and a run as a No.1 bestseller across multiple genres, *From Green to Blue* more than earns its acclaim. Whether you're a fan of police procedurals or simply enjoy character-driven narratives with heart, this is a standout read that lingers long after the final page. Cox delivers realism with charm—and that's a rare badge of honour.

THE TROUBLESEEKER

by Alan Lessik

A bold, lyrical journey blending myth and memory—The Troubleseeker is a masterful, moving tale of love and liberation.

In *The Troubleseeker*, Alan Lessik blends mythology, magical realism, queer identity, and political struggle into an unforgettable tapestry of divine intervention and human resilience. Set against the vivid backdrop of Havana, Cuba, the novel imagines a semi-divine Emperor Hadrian returning to Earth two millennia after his death to seek redemption by guiding a young boy, Antinio, through perilous challenges in his quest for freedom.

Hadrian, haunted by the loss of his lover Antinous, allies with gods from Greek and Santería traditions to aid Antinio. Yet each act of interference weakens his celestial powers, raising the stakes with every choice. As Antinio journeys from oppression towards the promise of the United States, Lessik explores themes of destiny, sacrifice, and love with lyrical poignancy.

This richly layered tale, inspired by the life of René Valdes, is both intimate and epic—equal parts political memoir and mythological fable. Lessik's prose is vibrant and often laced with humour, balancing the heavy realities of exile, identity, and repression. The novel's fusion of the sacred and profane, the mythic and the modern, invites comparisons to Gabriel García Márquez's *One Hundred Years of Solitude*, yet retains a voice entirely its own.

The Troubleseeker is not only a daring reimagining of queer history but a powerful meditation on the cost of liberation. Enthralling and thought-provoking, it's a novel that deserves both praise and reflection.

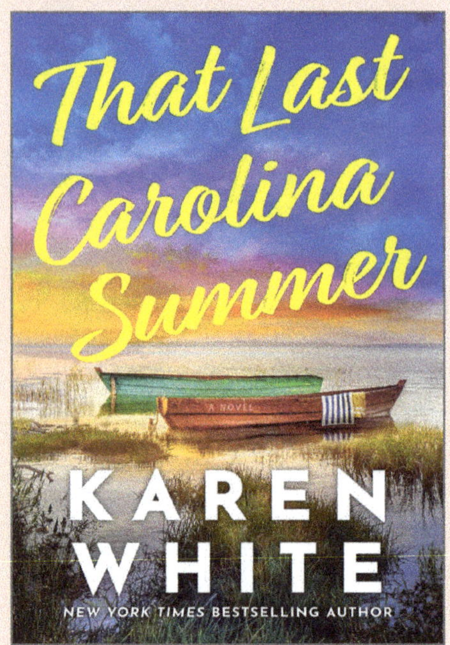

THAT LAST CAROLİNA SUMMER

by Karen White

Karen White masterfully crafts an emotional narrative filled with rich characters, gripping mysteries, and the enduring power of family bonds.

In *"That Last Carolina Summer,"* Karen White weaves a captivating tale that deftly explores the intricate tapestry of sisterhood, secrets, and the haunting grip of the past. Set against the lush, evocative backdrop of the South Carolina Lowcountry, the novel follows Phoebe Manigault, whose life takes a dramatic turn after she is struck by lightning as a child, gaining the gift of premonition.

Returning to Charleston to support her ailing mother, Phoebe is confronted not only by her complicated relationship with her stunning sister Addie but also by long-buried family tensions. White brilliantly captures the emotional turmoil and the sense of longing that defines Phoebe's journey, interweaving her narrative with the poignant story of Celeste, a woman still reeling from her granddaughter's mysterious disappearance. Their connection, forged through shared grief, adds depth to the unfolding mystery and highlights the theme of resilience in the face of loss.

Phoebe's introspective exploration invites the reader to ponder the weight of past choices and the paths to redemption. As her nightmares escalate, the tension mounts, leading to a shocking revelation that is both harrowing and redemptive.

White's lyrical prose and richly drawn characters ensure that *That Last Carolina Summer* is not just a story about returning home but also a profound meditation on the bonds that tie us together. This novel is a heartfelt reminder that while the past may haunt us, it can also offer the promise of healing and second chances. A truly unforgettable read.

SULTRY, IS THE NİGHT

by Barbara Avon

Barbara Avon's evocative prose, vivid imagery, and emotional depth make Sultry, Is the Night a hauntingly unforgettable read.

Sultry, *Is the Night* by Barbara Avon is an evocative tale that intertwines the complexities of love, loss, and personal transformation, set against the nostalgic backdrop of the 1980s. The narrative opens with the poignant death of a mother and the resulting emotional tumult experienced by her son, Mario. Avon adeptly captures Mario's grief and anger, presenting a vivid portrayal of a soul grappling with his past amid the chaotic remnants of a life barely lived.

The writing brims with rich imagery and emotional depth. Avon's deft use of language transports readers into a world resonant with both beauty and pain. From the haunting descriptions of the desolate cityscape to the intimate moments of despair and defiance, the prose evokes a visceral reaction, making it impossible to detach from the protagonist's journey.

Moreover, the novel skillfully navigates dark themes, including the struggle for belonging and the quest for self-acceptance. It reminds readers that love, no matter how messy, has the power to redeem and heal. Avon's exploration of these sensitive themes is both honest and poignant, reflecting her own views on life's complexities.

Ultimately, *Sultry, Is the Night* is not just a love story but a reflection on our innate desire to overcome challenges and connect with others. This first edition is sure to captivate those who appreciate narratives filled with nostalgia, emotional resonance, and the relentless pursuit of love. With a strong language warning and mature content, it is best suited for adult readers prepared to delve into the darker aspects of life and romance.

BEWEPT

by Colleen Coyne

Haunting, beautifully written, and deeply immersive. Bewept masterfully explores grief, memory, and suspense with poetic prose and psychological depth. Absolutely unforgettable.

Colleen Coyne's *Bewept* is a haunting and deeply emotional novel that explores the devastating impact of grief and the slippery nature of memory. The story follows Anna, a woman who has seemingly achieved her ideal life—only for it to be torn away in an instant. Her husband's sudden death catapults her into a profound mourning that warps time and distorts her sense of reality. But as the fog of loss thickens, it becomes apparent that something more sinister may be lurking beneath her sorrow.

Coyne's prose is both poetic and unflinching, drawing readers into Anna's fractured world with vivid detail and a sharp emotional edge. The novel does more than simply depict grief—it immerses the reader in its raw, disorienting power. The interplay between past trauma and present uncertainty is masterfully handled, keeping the tension taut as Anna's journey unfolds. The narrative is punctuated by moments of eerie suspense, making it difficult to determine whether Anna's mind is betraying her or if darker forces are at play.

One of *Bewept's* greatest strengths is its psychological depth. Coyne captures the terrifying possibility of early dementia with unsettling clarity, making Anna's fears feel as real as the ghosts that haunt her past. As the novel builds toward its gripping conclusion, each revelation is both heart-wrenching and satisfying.

Beautifully written and profoundly moving, *Bewept* is a compelling psychological drama that lingers long after the final page. A must-read for those who appreciate emotionally charged, thought-provoking fiction.

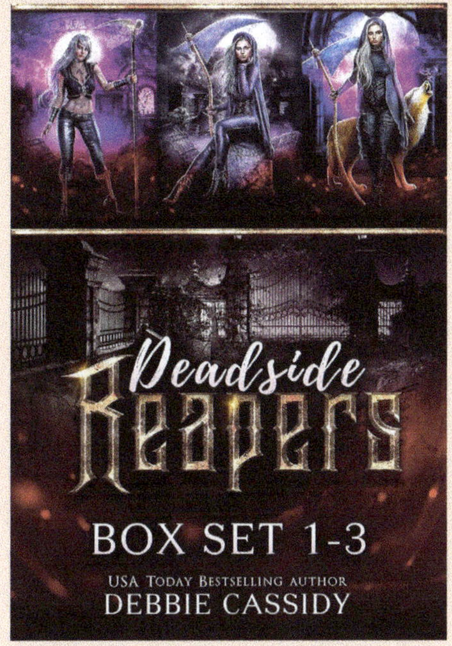

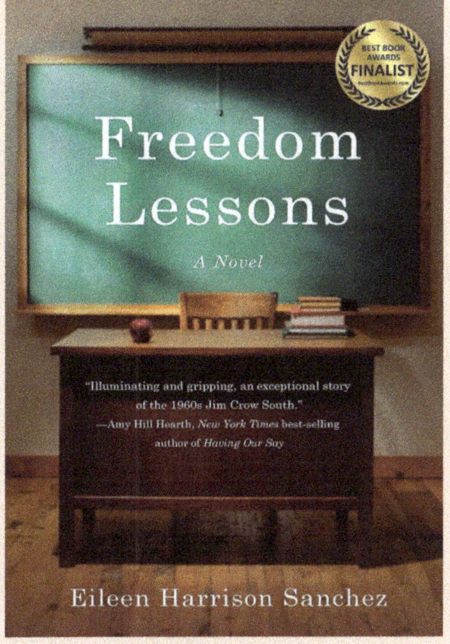

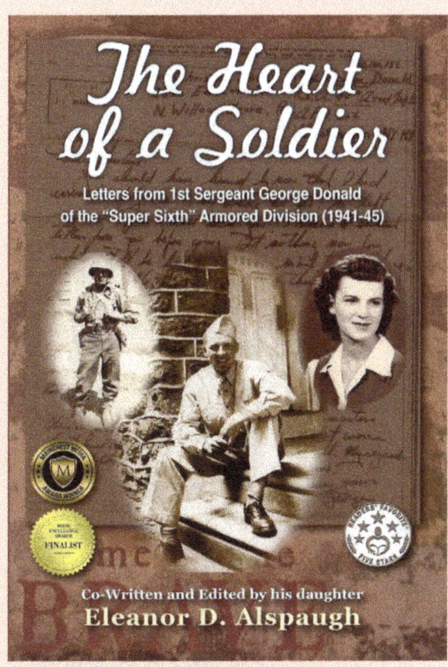

DEADSİDE REAPERS

by Debbie Cassidy

Thrilling, witty, and addictive! Deadside Reapers delivers sharp dialogue, intense action, and unforgettable characters in a brilliantly crafted urban fantasy world.

Debbie Cassidy's *Deadside Reapers* box set is an exhilarating urban fantasy trilogy packed with action, humour, and a touch of the supernatural. Bringing together *Reaper Unexpected, Reaper Uninvited, and Reaper Untamed*, this collection introduces us to a world where ghosts roam freely, reapers wield immense power, and one woman finds herself caught in the middle of it all.

The protagonist, a spirited soul relocation agent, is just trying to do her job—until she inadvertently inherits the scythe of one of Lilith's favoured reapers. This twist throws her into the path of three powerful and furious reapers, leading to a whirlwind of danger, intrigue, and undeniable chemistry. Cassidy masterfully balances intense action with witty banter, making for a fast-paced and addictive read.

The world-building is a standout feature, painting a vivid picture of Necro City and the supernatural hierarchy that governs it. The concept of Soul Savers Inc. is both intriguing and refreshingly original, blending the corporate and the macabre seamlessly. Fans of strong heroines will appreciate the lead's tenacity, while those who enjoy a slow-burn romance and sizzling tension won't be disappointed by the dynamic between her and the reapers.

With its sharp dialogue, gripping plot twists, and a dash of dark humour, *Deadside Reapers* is a must-read for urban fantasy lovers. Cassidy delivers an engaging adventure that keeps readers hooked from start to finish. If you enjoy a blend of supernatural drama and sass, this box set is well worth picking up.

FREEDOM LESSONS

by Eileen Harrison Sanchez

A powerful, heartfelt novel that captures the complexities of race, identity, and courage with authenticity, grace, and emotional depth.

Set against the backdrop of 1969 rural Louisiana, *Freedom Lessons* offers a poignant and deeply human narrative of integration, race, and resilience. Drawing from her personal experiences as a teacher during the civil rights era, Eileen Harrison Sanchez crafts a compelling story through the alternating voices of Colleen, an optimistic white newcomer; Evelyn, a seasoned Black teacher; and Frank, a high school football player shouldering the weight of his family's grief and survival.

What makes this novel resonate is its authenticity. The integration of schools is not just a historical event—it becomes a lived, messy, and emotional reality for each character. Colleen's journey is especially affecting as her initial naivety gives way to deeper understanding and difficult moral choices. Evelyn's perspective is equally powerful, challenging assumptions and revealing the complexities behind seemingly simple acts of resistance. Frank's story adds a youthful, raw layer of truth, showing the psychological toll systemic injustice can take.

Sanchez avoids caricature and instead offers nuance and heart. Her prose is simple yet evocative, perfectly suited to a story where small choices carry enormous weight. While the novel is steeped in a specific time and place, its questions—about justice, belonging, and what it means to do the right thing—are strikingly relevant today.

Freedom Lessons is a moving, thought-provoking novel that sheds light on an often overlooked moment in American history, reminding readers of the personal cost of change and the courage it demands.

THE HEART OF A SOLDİER

by Eleanor Alspaugh

A deeply moving and impeccably researched tribute to courage, resilience, and love amidst the horrors of World War II.

Eleanor Alspaugh's *The Heart of a Soldier: Letters from 1st Sergeant George Donald* is a deeply moving and meticulously crafted historical non-fiction work. Through a treasure trove of letters, the book offers a profoundly personal glimpse into the life of Sergeant George Donald, a soldier of the famed Sixth Armoured Division during the Second World War. His correspondence, often written under the duress of battlefield conditions, reveals a man of remarkable courage, humility, and devotion to both duty and family.

The letters, penned almost daily over the course of four years, capture not only the harrowing realities of war but also the enduring love that sustained Donald. His heartfelt words, full of vivid storytelling, bring to life the trials of General Patton's Third Army as it pressed from Normandy to the German Alps. They highlight his exemplary leadership, recognised by a Silver Star, a Purple Heart, and a Bronze Star, and underscore the human side of a soldier grappling with the horrors of combat.

Alspaugh complements her father's narrative with well-researched historical context, enriching the letters with insights into the broader scope of World War II, especially the challenges faced by the "Super Sixth." Her effort makes this book more than a collection of letters; it becomes a poignant tribute to the resilience of soldiers and their families.

Rich in historical detail and emotional depth, this book is essential for anyone with an interest in military history or a desire to connect with the human stories embedded within it. Highly recommended.

Aidan Mc Nally shares his journey from personal loss and addiction to becoming an acclaimed author, offering insights on resilience, self-discovery, and the transformative power of storytelling.

A Journey of Resilience and Transformation

AIDAN MC NALLY

EXPLORING LIFE'S HIGHS AND LOWS THROUGH WRITING

as told to Ben Alan

Aidan Mc Nally is a beacon of resilience and transformation, whose life story and literary works inspire readers to confront their own challenges with courage and introspection. Hailing from the quaint village of Loughshinny, Dublin, Aidan's journey is anything but small. His experiences have taken him across the globe, where he has embraced life's complexities with an unyielding spirit. Through his writing, Aidan invites us to pause, reflect, and realign our lives, offering a perspective that is both deeply personal and universally relatable. His ability to connect with readers on an emotional level is a testament to his authenticity and the profound impact of his words.

Aidan's literary contributions, including the award-winning "TWO sons TOO many," "17 & Life," and "Layman's Handbook," have garnered critical acclaim for their raw honesty and insightful exploration of the human condition. "TWO sons TOO many" is a poignant memoir that delves into the depths of personal loss and the arduous journey of healing, while "Layman's Handbook" provides practical tools for self-help and emotional growth. Aidan's works are a testament to his belief in the power of storytelling to heal and transform. His writing not only offers solace to those grappling with grief and adversity but also serves as a guiding light for anyone seeking to navigate the complexities of life with grace and resilience. Through his books, Aidan Mc Nally has established himself as a vital voice in contemporary literature, one that encourages us all to embrace our vulnerabilities and find strength in our shared humanity.

Aidan Mc Nally, award-winning author, shares his journey of resilience and transformation, inspiring readers worldwide with his powerful storytelling.

Your memoir TWO sons TOO many is a deeply personal account of your life, marked by incredible highs and devastating losses. How did the process of writing this book serve as a form of self-therapy for you, and what was it like to revisit such painful

"TWO sons TOO many" is a powerful, heart-wrenching memoir that beautifully captures resilience, adventure, and the strength of the human spirit.

memories?

Writing is believed to be therapeutic by many and I believed the same to be true. When writing about my own life story I found it very tough to write about the devastating loss that I have endured and not only once but twice in burying two of my sons. The process was at one time an 8 hour day at the keyboard where uncontrollable crying is all that I can recall. I never thought emotion could be communicated through text. The feedback to date has been, "thanks for making me cry so much", "I could not stop crying at this one part" to name a few. That was the part that was written in that eight hour day.

In Layman's Handbook: A Journey to SELF, you offer readers tools for self-help, self-care, and self-love. Can you share some specific strategies or practices from the book that have been most transformative for you in overcoming grief and finding joy again?

Grief is what we all know to be a funny/strange animal. Nobody wishes to experience this type of devastation or feeling of loss. What I call us to remember is that grief is a feeling and it will pass. And like all feelings it will come up again and again. The beautiful thing to remember is grief is love turned inside out. When we feel so strongly for somebody and then all of a sudden they are no longer there to receive our love, we grieve. Focus on how grief is born from our feelings of love. Take comfort in knowing that we can feel and we have love. This is a beautiful side of grief.

Aidan Mc Nally captivates readers with his authentic storytelling, offering profound insights into resilience, healing, and the human experience.

You describe yourself as a small village man with an appetite for life larger than the world itself. How has your upbringing in Loughshinny, Dublin, influenced your worldview and your writing, especially as someone who has travelled and lived in various parts of the world?

I always knew I was larger than the village where I grew up. A touch on a misspent youth showed all of the signs of this. I never understood that the world was my oyster when I was a teenager in my "hometown". When I did spread my wings to fly and travel to far away places I devoured that oyster they had all been telling me about in my youth. A side note, I cannot stomach oysters lol. All in all the village mentality and simplicity did serve me well when faced with turmoil on a much larger scale though.

Your journey from a troubled youth to a successful author is inspiring. How did your early experiences, including your struggles with addiction and time in prison, shape the man and writer you are today? What message do you hope readers take away from your story?

A saying in sobriety rooms and getting sober is "live life beyond your wildest dreams". I never though it to mean too much though. In writing my memoirs I was reflecting on a story of my life where I could not believe what had occurred in my own life. I was that soldier in all of those situations, both good and bad. For some areas in my story, I found it hard to believe and some might argue that parts have been a nightmare rather than any "wildest dreams" I can safely say the journey has been beyond my wildest dreams and that overcoming addiction in life helped lay the foundations inside of me that I drew upon when the real life hit the fan.The message is to never give up. Keep going because we never know what is next. In all of the bad times, know that in archery, the archer must pull the bow backwards before he can launch and hit the target.

Both of your books, TWO sons TOO many and Layman's Handbook, explore the themes of resilience and personal growth. How do you see the relationship between these two works? Are there common threads that tie them together, despite their different formats and focuses?

Both books are similar in the sense that they are all about myself and my findings and my experiences. In TWO sons TOO many, the reader will come along for an adventurous ride around the world filled with awesome experiences of mine and heartbreaking loss. In Layman's Handbook, the focus shifts from me, to joining me and exercising some simple tools and tips to help change our lives by exploring how I used or things that I found super useful to overcome emotional pains and difficult situations. I guess to say they are similar is only that the memoir is about my experiences and Layman's is how you can adapt what I have used in my own life to overcome your own situations as they occur for you. To be honest I felt guilty not to share all that I have learned an applied in my life as I know I would have wished for a helping handbook many times along my journey.

You mention that Layman's Handbook is intended to normalize discussions around mental health and emotional intelligence. What inspired you to write about these topics, and how do you hope your book will contribute to the ongoing conversation about mental health awareness?

I feel strongly about the subject as I could have been easily diagnosed with several conditions myself. Layman's Handbook takes a look at how stigma really means nothing. When we find a willingness inside of ourselves to delve into ourselves, it is then that we can begin to relax the mind and calm our emotions and begin to understand how we may only differ from others and we can put in work to thoroughly enjoy our lives. Understanding is the key and we cannot understand unless we experience. Some will say, "To love someone is to know them" and I will say "To know someone you must understand them". Who better to know than SELF?

Why should anybody take an interest or read any of your books?

I delivery a unique story of a boy turned man who overcame addiction. From a prison cell, to million dollar deal negotiations. A man who is as comfortably among celebrities and the elite as he is among the outcast or the homeless. We are all human first is a much more important insight than bank balance or status. Human nature is beautiful and reading my books will help any person to take a moment for themselves and cherish right where they are today. MY books offer the reader an insight of how anything IS POSSIBLE.

Exploring Family, Resilience, And The Power Of Storytelling

ALISON RAGSDALE

On Crafting Heartfelt Stories Rooted in Scottish Heritage and Emotional Truths

Alison Ragsdale discusses her Scottish-inspired novels, career transitions, and the emotional depth of her writing, offering insights into her creative process and advice for aspiring authors.

"Weaving the culture, the stunning scenery, and the grit and dry wit of the Scots into my books helps me feel close to home."

as told to Dan Peters

Alison Ragsdale, the acclaimed author of eleven bestselling contemporary women's fiction novels, has carved a unique niche in the literary world with her emotionally resonant stories set against the breathtaking backdrop of Scotland's Highlands and Islands. Her works, celebrated for their exploration of family dynamics, love, loss, and resilience, have garnered international acclaim and a devoted readership. From her debut novel, Tuesday's Socks, to her latest Kindle #1 bestseller, An Impossible Choice, Ragsdale's storytelling continues to captivate audiences with its depth and authenticity.

Born in Scotland and now residing near Washington D.C., Ragsdale's journey to authorship is as compelling as her novels. A former professional dancer and marketing executive, she turned to writing after a life-altering health diagnosis in 2009, using her experiences to craft narratives that resonate with raw emotion and universal truths. Her ability to weave the rich tapestry of Scottish culture and landscapes into her stories reflects her enduring connection to her homeland, even after decades living abroad.

In this exclusive interview for Reader's House Magazine, Ragsdale opens up about the influences behind her evocative novels, the challenges of transitioning careers, and the deeply personal connections she shares with her characters. She also offers invaluable advice to aspiring writers, encouraging them to embrace their voice and persevere in the face of obstacles. For fans of contemporary fiction and those curious about the creative process, this conversation with Alison Ragsdale is a heartfelt and inspiring read.

How has your Scottish heritage influenced the themes and settings of your novels?

Completely. All my books are set in the Highlands and islands of my homeland. I have lived overseas for over forty years, but my connection to Scotland has never waned. If anything, the separation has heightened my motivation to write about it. Weaving the culture, the stunning scenery, and the grit and dry wit of the Scots into my books helps me feel close to home, regardless of where I am in the world.

What was the most challenging part of transitioning from a career in ballet and marketing to becoming a full-time author?

Moving from dance to marketing was challenging because it was from necessity rather than choice. An injury put paid to my dance career before I was ready to give it up. Marketing happened almost by chance, thanks to a wonderful mentor who guided me to something he felt I could do well. From there, transitioning to writing was much easier because it fulfilled a life-long dream. That I can write every day now is a gift.

Your novels often explore deep emotional themes—how do you approach writing such poignant and heartfelt stories?

I approach it with care and lots of research. I am drawn in by emotionally charged stories, so it feels natural to write about them. I am acutely aware, however, of the sensitive nature of many of the subjects I tackle and how they might trigger or affect readers. I try to tread lightly while being accurate in my research and honest in my portrayal of emotions – writing from the heart.

Which of your characters do you feel the strongest connection to, and why?

This is a tough question because they all become like family to me. If I had to choose, I'd say Ailsa from The Art of Remembering. While her story is not my story it is as closely aligned to my experiences as I was comfortable writing. She is a complex character, strong and yet vulnerable, and it was fun to explore and develop her as she faced the ultimate challenge, when illness tears her away from a successful career that she has worked for all her life. I want to be Ailsa when I grow up.

Alison Ragsdale is a masterful storyteller who captivates audiences with her emotionally charged, authentic, and beautifully woven Scottish-themed novels.

What inspired the storyline of Her Husband's Child, and did you draw from any real-life experiences while writing it?

This story was inspired by a young woman I saw in a documentary. She had received a cochlear implant after an illness as a teenager caused her to lose her hearing, and her perspective on dealing with the effect that had on her life was fascinating. From there, I crafted my main character and wove the tale around her, adding elements of abandonment, adoption, and ultimately, the love that grows between a mother and the children in her care, regardless of genetics.

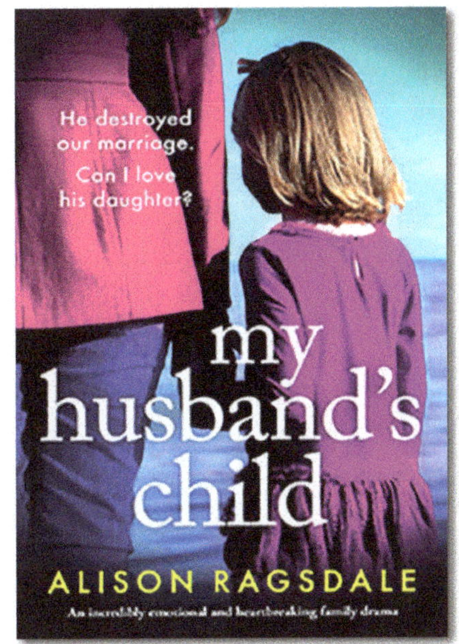

Alison Ragsdale's *My Husband's Child* is an emotionally gripping family drama exploring motherhood, love, and trust. With vivid characters and a compelling plot, it follows Cora's journey of resilience as she cares for abandoned children amidst mystery and conflict. A must-read for fans of heartfelt and suspenseful family stories.

What advice would you give to aspiring writers who want to break into the world of contemporary fiction?

Read as much of your chosen genre as you can, read some more, then start writing, whatever form it takes. Don't be daunted by all the potential obstacles, or dos and don'ts of technique or process, because that will paralyze you. Join a writing group if you can and begin to develop your voice. Connecting with other writers is always helpful, as the support of a trusted network can be invaluable in this business.

Exploring the Power of Reconciliation in Dystopian Fiction

Award-winning author CC Robinson discusses her gripping dystopian series Divided, the real-world experiences that shaped it, the challenges of crafting complex characters, and the vital role of hope in storytelling.

CC ROBINSON

INSPIRES READERS WITH THE DIVIDED SERIES AND A POWERFUL VISION OF HOPE IN DYSTOPIAN FICTION

by Z. Roberts I London

“I want Divided to inspire young people to fight against impossible odds, except with racial reconciliation at its core.”

CC Robinson is a storyteller of remarkable depth, weaving thrilling narratives that challenge, inspire, and ignite conversation. With a background as a medical doctor working in post-civil war nations and as a pastor in a diverse congregation, she brings a wealth of real-world experience to her fiction. Her work resonates with a rare authenticity, shaped by her firsthand encounters with resilience, hope, and the fight for justice.

Her young adult dystopian series, *Divided*, is a masterful blend of gripping storytelling and powerful themes. Set in a future where society has been fractured along ethnic lines, the series explores the cost of division and the courage required to resist oppression. The inspiration behind *Divided* stems from Robinson's own experiences, where she witnessed both the deep wounds of civil conflict and the extraordinary power of reconciliation. Now, with *Caged*, the highly anticipated second book in the tetralogy set for release in autumn 2025, she continues to challenge readers with thought-provoking questions about unity, identity, and the human spirit.

In this exclusive interview, CC Robinson shares the creative process behind her dystopian world-building, the challenges of crafting complex characters like Rose, and the research that brings her stories to life. She also offers valuable insights for aspiring writers who seek to craft socially relevant fiction.

Reader's House is honoured to present this conversation with an author whose work not only entertains but also dares to envision a better future.

What inspired you to write the Divided series, and how did your background influence the story?

An all-night dream started me on the journey of conceiving and then writing the Divided series. I saw our nation fight a civil war over racial issues and a drug lord-turned dictator take power and separate the remaining population into ethnic groups and lock them behind impregnable walls. Forty-five years later, teenagers grew up never having met someone from another ethnicity. I then met all four of my main characters — Marcos, Rose, Harriet, and Jason — and knew I needed to tell their freedom story.

My background as a physician working in post-civil war nations definitely impacted not only my writing, but how I weave courage, hope, and working together into these novels. Often, dystopian can be a dark genre, not at all hopeful. But the young adult dystopian greats, like Divergent, Maze Runner, or The Hunger Games, all inspired young people to fight against impossible odds. I want Divided to do the same, except with racial reconciliation.

Your books explore themes of division and resistance — how do you hope readers will connect with these themes?

I hope readers will recognize the seeds of division and hatred in our society and in their own lives. We have no hope of seeing racial reconciliation in the larger social context if we live our lives in ethnic silos. I want to show for young readers that, though it can be difficult, living a life of reconciliation with other ethnicities is worth the price.

CC Robinson masterfully blends thrilling narratives with profound themes, crafting unforgettable stories that challenge societal norms and inspire change through courage, resilience, and hope.

Can you share some details about your world-building process for the Federated Republic of America?

World-building is one of the most fun tasks I have as an author. I'm very strategic in my wiring, and building the world component by component is a therapeutic for me. I started with the governmental structure, with the division and isolation of ethnic groups as the central theme. Then I built the world outward — what would education look like in a regime wanting to maintain control over the population? What lies will youth need to believe in order to not push against the regime's control? What food will the regime allow each area to use, via a rations system? What items are available in each area's market? What does each area produce and why is that important? Is everyone allowed to pursue college or is that available for a select few? What role would an "election" have inside a regime controlled by a dictator? These questions and more have to be answered in the planning stages.

I craft the world's framework after I've firmed up the characters. I feel the characters and their transformations should drive both the world-building and the plot. But each world-building element, for instance, embedded chips in every citizen's forearm, has to make sense within the bigger plot picture (monitoring of movement) and characterizations (how the regime's control grates against their independence or not).

Sophie's journey in Deception takes her through nuclear-ravaged lands — what kind of research did you do to make these environments feel realistic?

I've traveled extensively through the area where Deception is set — the foothills of the Appalachian mountains — and I've visited a saltpeter cave much like the one in Deception. As far as the impact of nuclear weapons on the land, I dug into the post-Chernobyl history and how Japan recovered from the nuclear bombs of Hiroshima and Nagasaki to portray how long land takes to restore itself, if left alone. The short answer is the timeline for recovery depends on how far away the land in question is from the impact site, the patterning of fallout and prevailing winds / rainfall at the time of impact, and other geological features, such as mountain ranges or bodies of water.

What was the biggest challenge in writing Caged, and how does it expand on the themes introduced in Divided?

The biggest challenge in writing Caged was handling Rose's chaotic anger. As a main character, she's my most challenging, because I recognize my own faults in her. But also because Rose will take risks I would never dream of taking in real life. I had drafted the outline, and, while writing, Rose threw a complete curveball. I thought about her plot twist for a while and realized this was the best journey for her character growth. But this meant redrafting the entire back half of Caged.

How has your experience as a medical doctor and pastor shaped the way you write characters and their struggles?

My experience as a medical doctor working in post-civil war nations and as a pastor pushes me to weave hope and courage through everything I write. I've witnessed people in the lowest of low places — after a civil war and grieving their family's murder, or seeing people walk through the worst personal crises we could imagine. And yet, I've also seen those same people face their challenges with courage. One of the biggest elements for surviving the unthinkable evils of life is the strength of community and the person's unwavering faith. I bring these into my narratives, whether that's a full-length novel, a novella, or a short story.

Rose, now imprisoned and isolated, must escape before her captors' sinister plans come to fruition. As she uncovers their schemes, the stakes grow higher—not just for her, but for her entire city. With time running out, she must fight for freedom in this gripping YA dystopian sequel to *Divided.*

What are some of the dystopian books or authors that have influenced your writing style and storytelling?

I adore the "classic" young adult dystopian series from the early 2000s — Divergent, The Hunger Games, and Maze Runner. These absolutely influenced my writing and storytelling. But more recent works have also been an inspiration for me as an indie author, including KA Riley's The Cure Chronicles, Claire Littlemore's Flow, and Emma Ellis's Eyes Forward. These ladies proved that being an indie author in the young adult dystopian space was not only possible, but readers wanted more.

What advice would you give to aspiring authors who want to write thought-provoking dystopian fiction?

I would ask them, "what provokes you about our current society?" Then I'd tell them to craft a story and build a world where that societal ill is the controlling element. Add great characters and a heart-pounding narrative and readers will devour it.

The Unique Voice Behind Award-Winning Fiction

Diana Mercedes Howell discusses her late-blooming writing career, the creation of "*Wishes Are Free*," childhood influences, and her approach to crafting stories that resonate across generations.

DIANA MERCEDES HOWELL

SHARES HER JOURNEY FROM LATE BLOOMER TO LITERARY SUCCESS

“It was time to stop ignoring the signs. It was a now-or-never decision. Jump off the cliff and see if you can fly.”

Editot's Desk I London

Diana Mercedes Howell, the brilliant mind behind the universally acclaimed middle-grade novel *Wishes Are Free*, brings a refreshing perspective to children's literature that resonates deeply with readers of all ages. Her masterful storytelling, woven with threads of compassion, understanding, and the magical essence of childhood, has earned her a distinguished place in contemporary children's literature.

The remarkable journey of this California-born author, who embarked on her writing career at fifty-three, serves as an inspiring testament that creative pursuits know no age boundaries. Her debut novel, set in 1959 Campbell, California, masterfully captures the zeitgeist of an era when summer days stretched endlessly and children's adventures held unlimited possibilities.

Through our delightful conversation, Howell shares fascinating insights into her creative process, her childhood influences, and the universal themes that make *Wishes Are Free* such a compelling read. Her authentic approach to storytelling, drawing from real-life experiences and genuine emotions, creates a narrative that bridges generational gaps with remarkable ease.

As Editor of *Reader's House,* I am particularly struck by Howell's ability to craft characters that linger in readers' minds long after the final page is turned. Her protagonist, *Rose O'Reilly,* alongside the wonderfully drawn Grandpa, represents the perfect blend of innocence and wisdom that defines truly memorable children's literature.

We are honoured to present this exclusive interview with Diana Mercedes Howell, whose work reminds us that the best stories, like the best wishes, come from the heart.

What inspired you to write *Wishes Are Free*, and how did you come up with the idea for the story?

When I began writing fiction, I discovered I enjoyed making up children's short stories. In the beginning, my main character in *Wishes Are Free*, Rose O'Reilly, was a five-year-old named Sally. I read these stories aloud to my intellectually challenged BFF, April. She loved them, and I thought, "I may have something here." I linked those stories together, aged Rose/Sally by five years, added more stories and *Wishes Are Free* was born.

By linking these short stories together, Wishes is naturally episodic. There is an over-arching conflict, but each part is a mini-novel within the whole. So, I ended up with several stories in one book.

The over-arching theme, losing your best friend, was my only intentional idea for the book.

How did your childhood experiences influence the themes in your writing, particularly in "*Wishes Are Free*"?

Like anyone, there were good times and not good times growing up. Uncertainty ruled my upbringing. My father suffered from alcoholism and my mother dealt with depression. It was an atmosphere of shifting sands. The main theme of the book is misunderstandings. Rose's kind acts somehow backfire and she gets into trouble as did I growing up.

> Diana Mercedes Howell masterfully weaves compassion and childhood wonder into timeless stories that touch hearts and inspire young minds across generations.

All the fun stuff, slumber parties, trips to the beach, middle school crushes, making new friends, and Saturday Kiddie Matinees are there, too.

Could you tell us more about your decision to start writing seriously at the age of fifty-three? What motivated you to pursue this passion later in life?

It was time to stop ignoring the signs. It was a now-or-never decision. Jump off the cliff and see if you can fly.

I knew I was on the right path, an almost spiritual path. All is right with the world feelings enveloped me each time I sat down at the keyboard to put one word in front of another. Ironically, the first piece ever published was an essay entitled: "It's Never Too Late."

Do I regret not starting earlier? No. Things happen as they are meant to.

How do you approach character development, especially for young protagonists like Rose in *Wishes Are Free*?

Every character in *Wishes Are Free* is based on me or the people I encountered growing up; the kids in my old neighborhood, teachers and relatives. The characters most like me are Rose and Grandpa. Because my two sides are represented, it's part autobiographical.

What do you believe makes a children's story resonate with both young readers and adults?

Emotions are universal. Adult friends repeatedly use words like compassion, kindness, and heartwarming to describe *Wishes Are Free*. Many say they were reminded, in a delightful way, of their own experiences growing up. Reviewers, without exception, write that Wishes is a splendid read for any age.

Adults identify with Grandpa, and kids identify with Rose. Parents recognize themselves in the way he bonds with Rose and guides her through ten-year-old challenges. Whether children are lucky enough to have a kind adult guiding them, or not, they take to Grandpa's respect for his ten-year-old granddaughter. And how Rose deals with parents, teachers, bullies, and a big brother keep kids engrossed.

Wishes Are Free is optimistic. Each part ends with Rose writing her thoughts about what has happened in her diary. She draws her own conclusions, which makes her a good model for kids.

How do you incorporate your love of imagination into your writing process?

This is the fun part! I love the freedom to go wild. I have total control of the narrative within the boundaries of how my characters would naturally act and react.

Wishes Are Free opens in 1959 in Campbell, California. Geography is a given. For the rest, I usually start with dialogue. As ideas come to me, I'll add layer after layer of description, emotion, and reactions using the same method as Bob Ross the PBS landscape painter of the 70s. He would start with a sketch and add depth and dimension with countless strokes of his brush.

Innumerable edits, additions, and subtractions follow until I have created a vivid, entertaining scene that reads smoothly and moves me in some way.

Villains are the most fun to create. Their actions and words flow effortlessly from my imagination. I don't know why that is. Is there a part of me that would like to be a villain in real life?

> *Wishes Are Free* is a touching story about ten-year-old Rose dealing with her best friend's departure while bonding with her widowed grandfather. The book skillfully addresses themes of friendship, loss, and hope through authentic storytelling making it perfect for young readers while resonating with all ages.
> *Wishes Are Free, Be Careful What you Wish,* will be out this summer.

What advice would you give to aspiring authors who are just starting out or considering writing at a later stage in life?

If you can't not write, there's your cue. Choose a genre. What excites you? Romance? Thrillers? Mystery? Fantasy? Non-fiction? Poetry?

Write, write, write. Rewrite, rewrite, rewrite. Let "It isn't good enough" be your mantra. That is the only way your writing will be the best you have in you.

So when do you know if it's good enough? You will know. You will put it aside for a time and come back to it. Many times, the thought, "I wrote this? This is good!" will hit you. You're done!

Join critiquing groups. You will not regret it. For every misguided critique, there will be feedback worth its weight in gold.

Read, read, read. Read the best writing in every genre. Don't give up. Kate DiCamillo, renowned and prolific children's book author, endured 473 rejections before Because of Winn Dixie, which has now sold 10 million copies, was accepted by Candlewick Press.

A Soldier's Story, A Daughter's Perspective

Eleanor D. Alspaugh discusses weaving personal stories with historical research, the inspiration behind her award-winning books, and her passion for telling meaningful, heartfelt tales that transcend time and place.

ELEANOR D. ALSPAUGH

SHARES THE HEARTFELT STORIES BEHIND HER BOOKS AND THE LEGACY OF LOVE AND RESILIENCE

"My writing comes from my heart...sharing humanity in the challenges of life."

as told to Dan Peters

Eleanor D. Alspaugh is a name that beautifully resonates among lovers of heartfelt storytelling and true-to-life narratives. A multi-award-winning author, Eleanor masterfully weaves together deeply personal experiences with broader, universal themes, allowing readers to step into histories and lives that feel both intimate and pivotal. With a talent for unearthing profound lessons amidst the everyday, Eleanor's books—ranging from her laugh-out-loud insights into motherhood in *The Mommy-Go-Round*, to her poignant homage to military families in *When D is For Deployed*, to the richly detailed historical tapestry of *The Heart of a Soldier*—leave an indelible imprint on her audience.

In her latest triumph, *The Heart of a Soldier*, Eleanor achieves a remarkable feat: blending her father's personal wartime letters with meticulously researched historical context. Set against the backdrop of World War II, the book offers a window into the life of a soldier navigating love, duty, and danger, while simultaneously unfolding the human stories of those on the home front. The book has already garnered acclaim, including the 2023 Maincrest Media Book Award for Historical Non-Fiction and a Runner-up position in the 2024 Book Excellence Awards' Military Category—testaments to its brilliance.

Eleanor's work effortlessly embodies a balance between historical accuracy and emotional depth, reminding readers that history is not just about events, but about people: their love, sacrifices, and enduring humanity. Throughout her literary journey, she has maintained a strong connection to her roots as a proud wife, mother, grandmother, and storyteller, drawing inspiration from the lives of those closest to her.

In this exclusive interview, Eleanor takes us behind the scenes of her creative process, her inspiration for *The Heart of a Soldier*, and the legacy she hopes to leave through her writing. Whether you're drawn to history, personal reflection, or simply the honest truths of life, Eleanor D. Alspaugh's words promise to engage and inspire you deeply.

What inspired you to write "The Heart of a Soldier," and how did you approach combining personal letters with historical research?

Having saved my father's letters written home during World War II, my mother had often asked me to read the letters. I preferred just enjoying our visits and reminiscing of times when my father was still with us. However, once they were both gone, the letters became a lifeline to me, a way to reconnect with both my parents. As I read them, I felt moved by their story, and wanted to share the letters with others, particularly my family. Knowing how busy the world we live in is, I truly doubted that even my own family would find the time to open each envelope, see the personal notes tucked inside and read the letters filled with his experiences and heart. I also could not help but wonder what was going on in the world around them as they corresponded. It was then that I began to envision a book that included Dad's letters and some from my uncles, but also the history occurring as they wrote their letters. I felt others might enjoy the letters and learning about this historic time that my parents and so many others had lived through, presented in a personal manner rather than an impersonal history textbook. The book shares their story and at times, my thoughts as I entwined the letters with extensive research of significant World War II events and circumstances, in addition to sharing the combat path of my father's unit, the Sixth Armored Division of General Patton's Third Army.

Eleanor D. Alspaugh captivates readers with heartfelt storytelling, fusing historical insight and emotional depth into timeless, inspiring narratives of love and resilience.

How did your father's letters influence your understanding of his experiences during World War II and his relationship with your mother?

My father's letters shared the perspective of a wartime soldier, determined to do his duty, yet realizing he might never return to her. Although deeply in love, he was selfless, loving my mother enough to encourage her to keep living life, having fun, even dating. Dad stated that he would not marry her before leaving for the war as he did not want her to have to spend her life caring for him if he returned severely injured.

What challenges did you face while researching and writing about the historical context of your father's service in the "Super Sixth"?

As I started writing The Heart of a Soldier, I faced numerous challenges. I was a working wife and mother, raising three children, and had achieved my desired position as an Assistant Vice President, with an abundance of responsibilities and writing assignments that accompanied that title. I was also secretly working on my first book, writing nights, weekends, and vacations, what would eventually be my first award-winning book, entitled The Mommy-Go-Round. Oh yes, and there was one more 'little hitch' to my plan for this book. I was a business major and as far from a historian as one could get. I had to face facts and postpone further writing or research until about 15 years later, when I grabbed at the opportunity of an early retirement. My dream of writing this book was still in my heart.

How do you balance writing about deeply personal family stories with ensuring historical accuracy and broader appeal?

My writing comes from my heart. My first very personal book shared a naïve working mother's initiation into motherhood. It was fun, sometimes challenging and perhaps, in lieu of therapy, I worked through my thoughts, feelings and observations as I wrote that first book. I later wrote a second book, When D is For Deployed, again heart driven as I watched my son-in-law deployed, and his wife, my daughter, and their young daughter try to continue their everyday life yet stay close to him, despite being worlds apart. As for The Heart of a Soldier, I was always aware of my father's heroism and the medals he received for his service, but that was family history. When finally reading his letters and immersing myself in World War II history, my heart was touched as I was transcended in time, touched by my parents' love at its beginning, and began to see the challenges and struggles they endured at home and away as he fought in this war. Together, it all gave me a much better understanding of the impact on their lives, their hopes and dreams and I realized that so many other lives were also put on hold as they faced similar challenges at home and around the world.

What message or lessons do you hope readers take away from "The Heart of a Soldier"?

Everyday life is known to have stress and challenges. As I researched and wrote this book, I read so much of the various challenges, dangers and difficult circumstances soldiers and citizens faced during World War II. As a result, I tried to draw readers into their long-ago reality. I encouraged people to imagine what their lives would be like if subjected to those same prejudices and struggles, not to mention the danger faced in battle or even extensive training. I do hope that readers of The Heart of a Soldier will better understand the hardships people endured during World War II and the lasting love of family that helped soldiers survive.

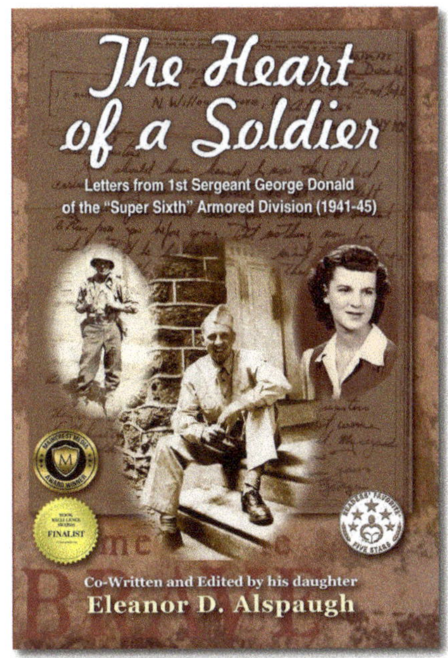

Eleanor Alspaugh's *The Heart of a Soldier* is a moving blend of personal letters and historical context, capturing Sgt. George Donald's bravery, sacrifices, and enduring love during World War II. Through intimate correspondence and supplemental research, the book offers a heartfelt tribute to the Greatest Generation and their wartime experiences.

Can you share any details about your upcoming projects, such as the sequel to "The Mommy-Go-Round" or your next children's book?

Occasionally, you will hear someone comment that parenting never ends. Well, let me assure you, that is absolutely true! I still find humor sharing life realities that parents experience as their children grow up, marry and eventually become parents themselves. The joy of parenting seriously includes so many unexpected situations that no one warns you about, so stay tuned! Both the sequel and my children's book are making progress. Hopefully, the chaos of parenting and grandparenting will not hold me back too long! Stay tuned!

From Poetry to Prose: The Evolution of a Storyteller

J.R. RICE

Shares His Journey, Writing Process, and the Power of Storytelling

J.R. Rice discusses his novel Broken Pencils, the impact of mental health on his writing, his experiences abroad, and the power of storytelling in connecting with readers on a profound level.

"I was his Black Jedi and he was my Beatnik Yoda."

as told to Z. Robers

J.R. Rice is a literary force whose work resonates with raw emotion, unflinching honesty, and a deep sense of purpose. An award-winning author, poet, educator, and spoken word artist, Rice brings a unique voice to contemporary literature, weaving together his personal experiences with the broader struggles of identity, mental health, and self-discovery. His critically acclaimed novel Broken Pencils has garnered prestigious accolades, including the 2024 Literary Titan Gold Book Award and the 2024 Pencraft Summer Best Book Award for Young Adult Coming-of-Age Fiction. As the first instalment in the Broken Pencils series, his poetry collection I Was, Am, Will Be expands on these themes, taking readers on a profound journey of transformation.

What inspired you to write about Jonah Tarver's journey in I WAS, AM, WILL BE?

After experiencing the traumatic loss of my father, a breakup with my ex-girlfriend, and being laid off from my teaching job, I left America to travel through Europe. I spent time in Greece and Spain, searching for purpose during a turbulent period in my life. I encountered incredible people and had unforgettable adventures that reshaped my perspective, which heavily influenced my poetry book I Was, Am, Will Be.

In the book, the reader follows Jonah Tarver from Broken Pencils, now a 25-year-old Black American on a three-month journey through Spain, Greece, France, and Amsterdam. Jonah embarks on a quest exploring determination, destiny, and death, taking the reader along on his heroic journey, continuing the Broken Pencils series.

How did your experiences abroad, particularly in Greece, shape your writing style and voice?

Living and studying in Paros, Greece, under the mentorship of George Crane, author of Bones of the Master, was a transformative experience. I was the Black Jedi to his Beatnik Yoda. He taught me about minimalism, emphasizing the importance of removing excess and giving purpose to every sentence, line, and word. This approach had a profound influence on my writing style and voice.

What role does spoken word artistry play in your creative process as a writer?

Spoken word artistry is integral to my writing because I incorporate elements like repetition, similes, extended metaphors, and rhythmic language into my novels to create an engaging experience for readers, especially when read aloud. Beyond writing, I use spoken word to build community, hosting and curating events like the local artist showcase series, SOCIAL SATURDAY, and organizing fundraisers in the Bay Area.

How do you balance your teaching career with your writing and artistic pursuits?

Balancing my full-time teaching job with my creative pursuits has been challenging. I work 40 hours a week as an English teacher and spend my free time writing, performing spoken word, hosting events, creating content, and more. While I feel skilled in each role, I often worry about becoming a "Jack of all trades, master of none," which creates anxiety about where to focus my time. It's a blessing and a curse to be talented in multiple areas, yet I often struggle with committing fully to one without feeling regret about the others. I remind myself of Henry Thoreau's quote: "My life has been the poem I would

JR. Rice's unparalleled ability to weave raw emotion and deep purpose into his stories makes him an extraordinary literary voice.

have writ. But I could not both live and utter it."

What challenges did you face while writing Broken Pencils, and how did you overcome them?

Writing Broken Pencils was deeply personal and challenging. Like Jonah Tarver, I struggle with bipolar disorder and have a history of mental health challenges, including depression, mania, panic attacks, and suicidal ideation. Initially, I aimed to highlight mental health from a young Black teenager's perspective. But as I worked on the book, I confronted my own traumas and reflected on the causes and effects of my struggles.

In recent years, I've prioritized self-care, regularly engaging in activities that promote mental health. Broken Pencils has had a profound impact on my life, helping me develop a deeper understanding and love for my imperfect but beautiful self.

Can you describe the significance of your characters' personal struggles in your novels?

In Broken Pencils, the protagonist, Jonah Tarver, a troubled Black teenager from Oakland, believes life is pointless, like a broken pencil. On the night of his senior prom and the anniversary of his best friend's death, Jonah embarks on a journey to find his purpose.

The story was inspired by my own struggles with mental health. I've battled depression and manic episodes since my teenage years, carrying the shame of not being understood. Through Jonah's journey, I wanted to explore the challenges of living with bipolar disorder, inviting readers to experience the emotional highs and lows, and ultimately, the beauty of embracing life's struggles.

Broken Pencils by J.R Rice is a powerful coming-of-age novel following Jonah Tarver, a troubled teen dealing with bipolar disorder and grief. Set over twelve hours in San Francisco, the book offers strong characterization and tackles mature themes with honesty, making it a compelling read for young adults.

What advice would you give to aspiring writers who want to make an impact with their work?

My advice is to stay authentic and true to your voice. Write from your experiences and emotions to connect with others across cultures and boundaries. Give a voice to the voiceless—the people whose stories show resilience through struggle. It's also vital to preserve the legacy of our ancestors by carrying their stories into the present, so future generations can do the same. This honors their sacrifices and triumphs while continuing their legacy.

EXPLORING THE HEART OF BAMPTILLIA

AN INTERVIEW WITH

LB HARPDOG

ON LOVE, LOSS, AND LITERARY CREATION

LB Harpdog discusses his unique Bampire mythology, the emotional inspiration behind MIND NIGHT BLUE, and how his writing explores love, loss, and the complexities of human relationships.

AS TOLD TO DAN PETERS

In the realm of speculative fiction, few authors have managed to weave the threads of personal emotion and imaginative world-building as seamlessly as LB Harpdog. With a unique voice that captures the heart and a storytelling style that defies convention, Harpdog has carved out a niche that is both deeply personal and universally resonant. His creation of the Bampires and the world of Bamptillia is a testament to his inventive spirit, offering readers a fresh take on the vampire mythos that is as intriguing as it is original. Harpdog's works are not just stories; they are emotional journeys that invite readers to explore the complexities of love, loss, and longing.

At the heart of Harpdog's writing is a profound exploration of love, most notably in his deeply personal work, MIND NIGHT BLUE. This narrative serves as a poignant love letter to his ex-girlfriend, Palmyra, and is imbued with the raw emotions of a love that transcends time and circumstance. Through his stories, Harpdog invites readers to experience the depth of his feelings, using his unique creations to express what words alone cannot. His ability to blend the fantastical with the deeply personal is a hallmark of his work, making each story a reflection of his own heart and soul. As you delve into this interview, prepare to be captivated by the mind and heart of LB Harpdog, a storyteller whose passion for his craft is matched only by his passion for the one who inspired it all.

You've created an entirely new creature, the Bampires, and a unique world, Bamptillia. Can you tell us more about the inspiration behind these creations and how they differ from traditional vampires? What drew you to develop this new mythology?

This is a 6 book series. I was inspired because of a broken heart. I wanted to tell my ex-girlfriend how much I truly loved her and what I couldn't say. Bampires helped me do it. Bampires originated from off world. They only survive by a virgins mind or body. But on Earth, they drink blood to endure Earth's atmosphere. Because on Bamptillia, they don't have any suns in their solar systems, only moons. So their eyes adapted with being an electric blue hue that allows them to see as if it were daylight to humans.

Virgins on Bamptillia are rare and used as a valuable source to prolong their lives. But they learned that Earth has an abundance of virgins. Plus the gravity on their home planet is very heavy. But on Earth, they are stronger, faster, and can fly because of the difference in gravity as well as the use of the mind that helps halfbreeds, Aka Vampires, to also fly and enter a person'smind when touching them and seeing their thoughts or controlling another person's thoughts.

LB Harpdog, the visionary author behind the Bampires series, shares his passion for storytelling and the personal journey that fuels his work.

I developed the Bampire ideas because no one knew how the first Vampire, Dracula, was created and when. So I created Bamptillia and a backstory to go along with the Vampires origin. And as far as them being extremely sexual, I wrote this book to reassure my ex-girlfriend that I truly did love her. But the initial story was very depressing. So I added an erotic flavor to make it interesting. But I may have gone a bit overboard with the sex, because I was challenged to write a story with a sex scene in every chapter, . So I did. Then I incorporated the sex into the origin of Bampires.

This was supposed to be a one off book. But turned into a 6 book series. Because I wanted more depth to the characters and so did my beta readers.

MIND NIGHT BLUE is a deeply personal work for you, written as a way to express your feelings for your ex-girlfriend. How did channeling these emotions into a fictional story help you process your experience, and what do you hope readers take away from

"MIND OF NIGHT BLUE" captivates with its gripping narrative and vivid characters. A masterful blend of suspense and emotion, it immerses readers in a hauntingly beautiful world. An unforgettable reading experience!

this story?

Palmyra and I had an untouched emotional affair. It was forbidden, because we had our own families. We never intended to date or fall in love. But I was planning to end my life and she was the only person who saw signs and talked me out of it by making her a few promises. Promises like: writing a story about our love, writing a song, traveling to Berlin (even if we were no longer speaking), me taking care of her financially (giving her 20,000 euros and creating the Bampire brand and giving it to her), and traveling...

I hope the readers take away that, true love is not selfish or breaks up families. That the ultimate sacrifice for me is giving the person you love what they need (Palmyra's was her family) and not what they want (I knew she wanted me but was conflicted). That loving someone from a distance is ok no matter how much it hurts. Know when to let go.

The concept of MHSTY, My Heart Sings To Yours, is a beautiful and intimate expression. How does this concept of love and connection play a role in your stories, particularly within the complex relationships you explore in MIND NIGHT BLUE?

LB Harpdog masterfully blends emotion and imagination, creating captivating stories that resonate deeply with readers and redefine speculative fiction.

Online, those 5 letters was how we knew it was us talking. In the story, Palmyra knew LB still loved her when he said MHSTY. If he never used those words, then she knew he never loved her. No one except LB and Palmyra knew why those letters were so important and what they meant, not what they stood for.

MHSTY means: I loved her with all my heart and she loved me. It deeply meant we were soulmates and that our love was real no matter where life takes us, and it took us in different directions.

The Bampire society you've created is described as being driven by pleasures and desires, yet they crave something that humans have—true love. How do you explore the tension between carnal desires and the deeper need for emotional connection in your writing?

Bampires have sex to live a long time. Yes it does feel good, but they must do it to survive. So they can get bored with just the act alone. When they fall in love, sex takes second place to getting to know that person. When they fall in love, they gain abilities to help them accomplish that continued love.

So in the story, everyone is having sex. But Attacker has sex to try to win LB's love. But LB didn't want sex from Palmyra, just to be with her in the moment. Yes, he did desire to have sex with her, but he wanted to know the secrets Palmyra's heart held and to know her flaws and all. So his time spent with her was less sex and more talking. But Attacker's point was more sex and less talking and try to take what she wants.

You mentioned that your writing style is unique and aims to capture the reader's heart. Can you elaborate on your approach to writing and how you ensure that your readers feel deeply connected to your characters and their emotions?

My writing style focuses on a subject that we deal with daily. Example: Cheating, death, and even feelings of regret and falling in love.

I tease them with a video book trailer. To get them interested in the story.

When they read, I place them in a scene and then unravel the story slowly. Then help them to understand the state of mind the characters are in. Then try to get the reader to think about how they would have handled that situation. Then I use very expressive words along with music from my Spotify playlist to really draw the reader in by having the lyrics speak to the reader along with the story being told.

To me, pain is the number one emotion that holds the most memories. Next comes pleasure, Then comes laughter. So I focus on telling a story with the first two emotions to suck in the readers with pain and hold them there with pleasurable scenes.

But I also show the view points of the characters at different times to show the reader why they acted a certain way.

So I try to capture:

MIND: marketing, videos, and direct offers for people to read it.

BODY: getting the reader angry, excited, or turned on.

HEART: Share the story of a broken creature who is put into a decision to choose between a promise, or his emotions. MHSTY is what connects the readers to a term of endearment when they see those 5 letters and is what I want people to wear and adopt as a sign of true love. I hope it makes them want a love like the one I experienced with Palmyra.

Your Time To Play series features short erotic stories that emphasize women's desires. What inspired you to write this series, and how do you hope it resonates with readers, particularly in terms of addressing the stigma around women expressing their sexual desires?

Time to Play series was written for Palmyra when we were dating online. Since I couldn't be there physically, I wanted to be there mentally. So I wrote those stories to share with her when she was in the mood to be with me. The 1s, and 2nd books were just short stories to put her in a frame of mind for desires since she didn't feel sexy.

But the last book was one that I wrote specifically for her. This story took about 6 months to write. It is a choose your desire story. You can read it 4 times and get different endings. I wanted her to know that with me, I would have made our love life very interesting. I am not the kind of man that people can figure out. So my story to her had to reflect this.

As far as the stigma goes, women already have men that they love in their lives. So many times the sex is lacking imagination. So my hope is that this helps them to quinch that desire by reading my books and maybe sharing this with their partners and having a discussion about sex and how both parties can be happy.

But for single ladies, I want the last book to be as if I am the man in your life for one evening while you read it. I want you to enjoy reading it many times until you reach your sexual satisfaction. Because we all need someone in our lives, even if it just one night.

Behind the Scenes of Delicious Surrender

Luce Sutherland discusses her inspirations, the grumpy-sunshine dynamic in Delicious Surrender, her approach to writing compelling erotic romance, self-care rituals, and her future book plans, including an exciting return to Scotland.

LUCE SUTHERLAND

BRINGS PASSION, POWER, AND SEDUCTION TO THE PAGE WITH HER AWARD-WINNING EROTIC ROMANCES

by Dan Peters I London

"I wanted to create an intense exchange that would grab the reader by the throat and not let go."

Luce Sutherland has long been a master of weaving passion, power, and raw emotion into stories that captivate the senses and set hearts racing. An award-winning author, she has carved out a space in the world of erotic romance that is both daring and deeply resonant. Her works are not just about desire—they are about the intricate dance between dominance and surrender, the pull of attraction that defies logic, and the kind of love that burns fiercely yet feels entirely real.

With *Delicious Surrender*, Sutherland delivers a masterclass in tension and chemistry, bringing to life the irresistible dynamic between Gage MacLeod, the brooding alpha, and Brynne, the fiery, sunlit force who challenges him at every turn. Her storytelling is unapologetically bold, filled with depth, intelligence, and that perfect balance of spice and soul. But beyond the pages, Luce is a passionate advocate for living life to the fullest—her motto, *"LIVE LIFE JUICY,"* is as much a philosophy as it is a way of writing.

In this exclusive interview, she opens up about her inspirations, her meticulous approach to storytelling, and the sensual artistry that makes her novels impossible to put down. From the secrets behind her grumpy-sunshine dynamic to the intoxicating pull of her book soundtracks, Luce Sutherland takes us behind the scenes of her literary world—one where pleasure, power, and passion collide in the most exhilarating ways.

What inspired the grumpy-sunshine dynamic between Brynne and Gage in Delicious Surrender?

It has recently occurred to me that I created characters that mirror my own life! Yes, I love reading about this kind of dynamic in romance stories, but this question had me examining my own relationship. Coincidentally, I have a grumpy alpha husband who can be ornery and opinionated, and I am the sunshine character who sees the bright side in everything. He has a multitude of wonderful qualities like Gage. Along with a brilliant mind, and steadfast integrity, he is deliciously handsome, and he often hides his soft and caring side beneath a bit of bluster. They say, write what you know, and I guess I did!

Which scene was the most challenging for you to write, and why?

The most difficult scene to write was the climax of act three. I wanted to create an intense exchange that would grab the reader by the throat and not let go. Crafting that highly suspenseful altercation was challenging and exciting once I found the right mix of distress, terror and shock for my hero and heroine. I cannot say much more than that, as the element of surprise is the best part.

> Luce Sutherland masterfully blends passion, depth, and irresistible chemistry, creating compelling stories that enthral readers with unforgettable characters and sizzling, emotional storytelling.

What real-life experience or research contributed the most to your portrayal of the BDSM lifestyle in the novel?

If I revealed my google search history, you would see the depth of my online research. I have also read all the classics – The Story of O, Anne Rice's Exit to Eden and the Sleeping Beauty series, Fifty Shades, Bared to You and at least twenty Black Lace novels. I'm not admitting to seeking out hands-on experience like my character Brynne.

If Delicious Surrender were adapted for television or film, who would you ideally cast as Brynne and Gage?

Great question! I see Theo James as Gage MacLeod. He is English, has the right look, and is super sexy. For Brynne, there are several natural redheads who could fit the role: Emma Roberts, Jane Levy, or Holland Roden.

You mention self-care as important to your creative process—can you share one self-care ritual you practise during intense writing sessions?

Massage Therapy. Spending hours at the keyboard can wreak havoc on my shoulders, neck and lower back. During a ninety-minute massage, I let my brain wander. Before I close my eyes, I focus on the next scene in the story. When I come out, I usually start typing the ideas into my phone immediately. I reach a higher state of creativity when I can quiet the noise of everyday life.

The book playlist includes a variety of songs—how did music influence your storytelling process?

When I was originally drafting the book, I put a different song at the start of every chapter. I chose some of my favorite artists and songs that conveyed the right energy for the upcoming scenes. Some of the songs are meant for Brynne – such as Alanis Morrissette, Sia and Ellie Goulding. The darker, more rock inspired songs are meant to convey Gage's heavier persona: Imagine Dragons, Niall Horan, and Joe Cocker. When my word count grew out of control, those were the first things to be slashed. Once I completed the book, I added my top favorites back and created a Spotify playlist for the book.

Is there a character or storyline from Delicious Surrender that you'd like to explore further in a future book?

Yes, definitely! After I complete the trilogy, which focuses first on Gage, followed by his two best friends, Cole and Aaron, there is a fourth book I've been thinking about. Mistress Patricia Valentine is getting her own story and I'm calling it The Hellcat Club. I'm excited because it will take us back to Scotland.

What advice would you give to fellow authors who want to write compelling erotic romance that balances spice, depth, and believable relationships?

Some recipes must be created in a certain order. I'm reminded of a cake recipe that requires prepping the dry ingredients first in their own bowl and blending the liquids separately. Then you fold them carefully together – little by little. My book roadmap is similar.

My advice is to start by creating compelling characters. Decide what will bring them together. If they start out as enemies, how will they overcome that initial dislike for each other? I spend several days creating character bibles for all the key players, then I set that aside.

Next, I plan an intricate plot that has plenty of twists and turns. I may not know every disaster that will befall my heroine, but I know there will be plenty of detours along the way. Finally, the most important ingredient is the spice!

For me, friction and chemistry are critical elements in a spicy story. As a reader, I don't want to wait too long to feel that attraction and see it building. An erotic romance needs temptation, seduction, sizzle, and emotions that start out simmering and end up boiling to the surface. The plot should carry the story. The characters must be compelling and layered, and the spice should singe the pages. Just like the cake, too much spice (or sugar) can ruin the recipe. Too many intensely passionate scenes can take away from the story. So, sprinkle it within the first three chapters and continue onward with careful moderation.

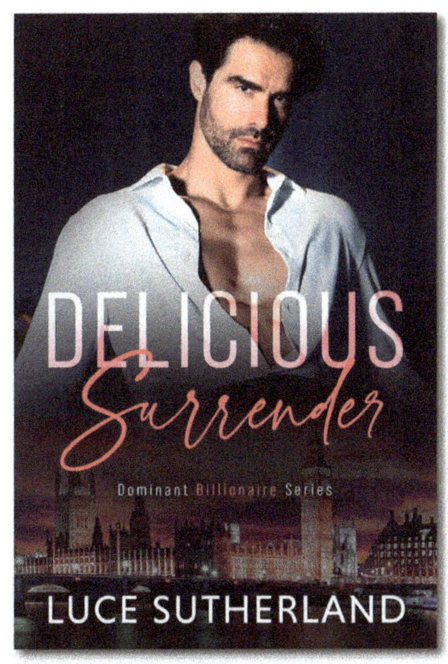

Delicious Surrender by Luce Sutherland is a steamy grumpy-sunshine romance featuring Brynne, an independent writer, and Gage, a domineering billionaire club owner. Their fiery attraction leads to conflict, betrayal, and high-stakes tension. With suspense, passion, and a hard-fought HEA, this captivating novel delivers spice, angst, and an irresistible power struggle.

A Life of Adventure, Writing, and Endless Imagination

Matthew Hughes discusses his influences, writing process, and love for morally complex characters. He shares insights on dialogue, world-building, and genre-crossing storytelling, offering a glimpse into his captivating creative mind.

MATTHEW HUGHES

A MASTER OF FANTASY, CRIME, AND SPACE OPERA

"A minor streak of criminality runs through my extended family, so when characters emerge, they tend to be on that side."

by Dan Peters I London

Matthew Hughes is a masterful storyteller whose works bridge the realms of fantasy, space opera, and crime fiction with a singularly rich voice. With an astonishing literary career spanning 24 novels and over 100 works of short fiction, his contributions to speculative fiction are nothing short of legendary. Whether crafting intricate worlds reminiscent of Jack Vance's Dying Earth or weaving compelling narratives filled with morally complex antiheroes, Hughes has consistently delivered fiction that is both intellectually engaging and deeply entertaining. His latest novels, *Margolyam* and *Henchmen*, further cement his place among the greats of the genre, offering readers a dazzling mix of wit, intrigue, and boundless imagination.

A recipient of the Endeavour, Global Book, and Arthur Ellis Awards, and an honouree of the Canadian Science Fiction and Fantasy Association's Hall of Fame, Hughes has earned the admiration of readers and critics alike. His literary career, however, is far from conventional. From writing speeches for Canadian government ministers to travelling the world as an itinerant housesitter, his life experiences have shaped the depth and authenticity of his storytelling. His sharp dialogue, layered plots, and keen observations on human nature make his work resonate across genres and generations.

In this exclusive interview, we delve into the creative mind behind *Henchmen* and *Margolyam*, exploring Hughes's literary influences, his intuitive approach to storytelling, and the fascinating journey that has brought him to this point in his career. Whether you are a longtime fan or a newcomer to his work, prepare to be inspired by one of the most original voices in modern speculative fiction.

Your works have often been compared to Jack Vance's; what is it about his writing that particularly resonated with you as a young reader?

I was thirteen, out on a farm with no bookmobile. I read anything I could get my hands on, including science fiction paperbacks my eldest brother left lying around. I read "The Dragon Masters" in Galaxy Magazine and was captured immediately. The premise was fascinating, and the plot moved quickly, but I think what caught me was what I can only call the coolness of the mood. That resonates with me still.

***"Henchmen"* features two characters navigating morally ambiguous situations—what interests you about exploring ethical complexity in your storytelling?**

I am, at heart, a crime writer. I fell into writing specfic by a series of flukes. A minor streak of criminality runs through my extended family, so when characters emerge from the back of my head, they tend to be on that side of the blanket. Also, I came of age in the 1960s, when antiheroes were all the rage. They seem to have stuck with me.

Matthew Hughes is a literary genius, seamlessly blending wit, adventure, and rich storytelling across fantasy, crime, and science fiction genres.

How did your previous career as a speechwriter influence your approach to crafting dialogue and narrative structure in fiction?

I spent decades writing for the voice, so I'm comfortable straddling the middle ground between formal prose and the way people actually talk. Good dialogue exists in that space.

I suppose I developed an innate sense of narrative structure from reading all my life, everything from Hemingway to Thorne Smith. Then, in my thirties, I spent some time as a script reader for Telefilm Canada and developed an understanding of story mechanics.

You've travelled extensively as a housesitter; how has experiencing different cultures directly impacted your world-building and character creation?

It's taught me that the little things make the difference. Like, if you're sitting in an Italian dentist's waiting room with other patients and a new one comes in, he will say Buon giorno to the group and they will all answer back. In Canada, we're liable to call a waiter "buddy." In France, you had better say, "Monsieur" unless you want something unwholesome in your soup.

***"Henchmen"* blends classic fantasy elements with your distinct sense of humour—how do you balance these tones while maintaining narrative tension?**

Intuitively, I suppose. I have a sense of rhythm that tells me when to insert a little lightness. Also, my characters seem to have inherited from me a sense of irony.

Your novels often feature complex societies and layered intrigues; how extensively do you plan your novels before beginning to write?

Not at all. I'm a pure-bred pantser. I start with a character, give him/her a problem, then see how they react. Other characters come into the action, with their own agendas, and I see where it goes. It all happens organically.

I'm writing a space opera right now. I sent the main character back to the world he fled from twenty-some years before. The backstory that has emerged as I push the action forward actually surprised me. I still don't know, a third the way through, how it's going to end.

You've achieved recognition across multiple genres and mediums—what drives you to continue pushing boundaries in your writing?

Do I? As I say, I'm a crime writer, so I write about thieves, forgers, burglars, henchmen, because they populate the back pastures of my mind. I think of myself as a decidedly old-fashioned kind of author, writing SF and fantasy that would have been publishable in the pulps and paperbacks of decades ago.

What practical advice would you give to other authors who aspire to build a sustainable career in speculative fiction?

Only the most generic, I'm afraid. I have not read science fiction or fantasy, except for Jack Vance and Gene Wolfe, since the mid-eighties. I have no idea what's current in the field today.

So the best advice I can give is: don't write plots and try to slot characters into them. You'll end up with a lame puppet show. Story comes out of character and plot comes out of story.

To demonstrate: last August, Fantasy Magazine published a little story of mine called "What's in a Name?" It's a retelling of a classic fairy tale, but because it's told from the point of view of a central character different from the original, it's a completely different story.

Vunt, a gambler, and Oldo, a farm boy, take a suspiciously well-paid warehouse job, uncovering criminal activity. Drawn into espionage for the Vanderoy wizards' Guild, they become caravan guards, navigating a perilous journey through magical cities, the Underworld, and dangerous schemes, facing powerful sorcerers and uncovering deep, hidden mysteries.

Seeking Truth Through Writing and Reflection

Michael Goddart shares his spiritual journey, the significance of past lives, meditation, and love in self-realisation. He offers wisdom for aspiring authors and insights from his experiences with enlightened teachers.

MICHAEL GODDART

INSPIRES READERS WITH PROFOUND SPIRITUAL INSIGHTS AND A JOURNEY OF SELF-REALISATION

“

Love plays the supreme role in the journey towards spiritual enlightenment. Our essence is love.”

Editor's Desk I London

Michael Goddart's literary and spiritual journey is nothing short of extraordinary. A revered author and seeker of truth, his works have garnered multiple prestigious awards, including the Nautilus Book Award and the National Indie Excellence Award, reflecting the profound impact of his writings. With a lifelong commitment to meditation and self-realisation, Michael has dedicated himself to guiding others towards a deeper awareness of their true essence.

His latest book, *The Contentment Dividend: Meditations for Realizing Your True Self*, is yet another testament to his ability to blend profound spiritual insight with practical guidance. Readers familiar with his previous books, *A New Now* and *In Search of Lost Lives*, will recognise his signature depth and clarity as he explores the pathways to higher consciousness. His memoir, which recounts the vivid details of 88 past lives, offers an unparalleled glimpse into the spiritual evolution of the soul—a subject that he approaches with remarkable authenticity and wisdom.

In this exclusive interview, Michael shares the inspirations behind his spiritual journey, the lessons he has gathered from his teachers, and the role love plays in our path to enlightenment. His insights serve as both a beacon of hope and a call to embrace the higher dimensions of existence. Whether you are a long-time practitioner of meditation or simply beginning to explore the vast realms of spiritual growth, Michael Goddart's words will leave you enriched, enlightened, and eager to embark on your own journey towards self-realisation.

What inspired you to begin your spiritual journey at such a young age?

Recent past lives prepared and primed me to seek my current spiritual path at such a young age. Twelve past lives back, when I was a very high-up government official, through my association with two Tibetan Buddhist monks I realized that humans have the potential to attain a higher consciousness that sweeps up through the heavens. As my past lives progressed, I was a priest in Prague, then a monk in Slovenia, then an Indian business owner who practiced raja yoga. When I served as a banker in Bombay during the Raj, I met a God-realized Saint, and that turbocharged my search for a true living Saint this current lifetime.

How have your experiences in different countries influenced your writing and spiritual teachings?

Having traveled in over fifty countries and worked in twenty, my greatest impression is that in actuality, we are all one and, at heart,

> Michael Goddart is a visionary author whose transformative works inspire seekers to embrace self-realisation, higher consciousness, and a life of spiritual fulfilment.

all want the same thing—love. However positively or negatively expressed or masked. These life experiences have inspired my calling to share spiritual truths with readers and listeners to empower them to lead lives of increasing awareness, bliss, and love.

Can you share a significant lesson you learned from one of your spiritual teachers in India?

The lesson that is driven home again and again is that we have been given the most precious gift—our human life. We were born to realize our fullest potential. That is self- and God-realization. Now is our time to evolve and mature spiritually.

What do you believe is the most common misconception people have about meditation?

The main misconception is actually a lack of understanding and appreciation that meditation can lead to an existence of unalloyed joy and wonder. Also, to truly meditate you need a living Teacher or Guide who is one with the One, who has realized their divinity, and who can initiate you into the practice of meditation on the Sound Current (aka Word, Holy Ghost, Logos, Shabd).

In your book In Search of Lost Lives, how do you think understanding past lives can impact one's current life?

Understanding your past lives can first, reveal the causes and reasons for inexplicable aspects of your life. Second, it can illuminate why you've felt immediate feelings of closeness with persons you meet and then get to know them readily because you've known them in past lives. It can also resolve and dissolve unwarranted aversions and dislikes. More important, through recovering and knowing the main trajectory of your past lives, you can begin to see and understand your individual journey, that of a spiritual being having human experiences. Knowing key past lives can illuminate experiences that furthered your spiritual evolution but also your devolution.

What role do you think love plays in the journey towards spiritual enlightenment?

Love plays the supreme role in the journey towards spiritual enlightenment. Our essence is love. That is who we truly are. Loving consciousness is the wisdom to awaken to and learn. We are born to learn to love, to realize true love as best we can, and we have the opportunity to return to Love via the soul's realization of increasingly higher and purer states of consciousness. But we get lost in everything else; the mind loves its diversions, its immersions, its benders, all to forget the self, that spark of immortal love. If we are evolving towards Love, we are shedding our ego and downward, outward tendencies and becoming purer, higher, more loving, more awakened in LoveSource. That is the name I write for the One that is nameless.

What advice would you give to aspiring authors who wish to write about spirituality and personal growth?

Identify with being a seeker after Truth. When asked similar questions in my interviews, I say that to be a seeker is the highest calling. Read widely. Meditate. Use your innate intuition to suss out the truth. Embrace your calling that you are on your path of spiritual evolution in the process of self-realization. In A New Now, in the meditations "The Wisdom of Seeking God" and "The Joy of Becoming," I write about the seeker's path. If you are an aspiring author, write daily if you can. Develop your higher knowing to discover what to write. Even if you don't aspire to be an author, you can write in a Journey Journal about your experiences of awakening further and making best use of your life.

Michael Goddart's *The Contentment Dividend* offers 49 meditations guiding readers toward spiritual self-discovery, inner peace, and divine connection. Rooted in teachings from realised Masters and Saints, it helps quiet the mind, access higher wisdom, and cultivate contentment. The book encourages reflection, receptivity to grace, and a deeper understanding of existence.

Crafting Compelling Tales Of Horror

PAUL J JACKSON

Captivates Readers With His Masterful Blend Of Suspense, Horror, And Thrills

Paul J Jackson discusses his journey in horror fiction, drawing inspiration from grief and personal experiences. His works blend supernatural and psychological elements, earning acclaim from Shaun Hutson.

By Editor's Desk

Paul J Jackson is a true testament to the power of perseverance and passion in the world of storytelling. Born on a leap year's day in the heart of the West Midlands, his journey as a self-published author is as captivating as the narratives he weaves. From the humble beginnings of jotting stories during a brief illness, to rediscovering his creative spark years later in the midst of family encouragement, Paul's path to literary success is one of resilience and inspiration. His works delve deep into the psychological and supernatural, exploring grief, vengeance, and the complexities of human emotions—all while keeping us on the edge of our seats, eagerly awaiting the next twist.

Paul's stories leave an indelible mark on the literary landscape, blending suspense, horror, and thrills with a masterful touch. His critically acclaimed novella, *Retribution: The Birth of a Horrifying Urban Legend*, showcases his exceptional ability to create gripping plots and unforgettable characters, earning him a 5-star rating and a gold award from Literary Titan. His anthology *A Pound of Flash*, a collection of 50 flash fiction stories, demonstrates his talent for crafting concise yet compelling narratives, while his anthology *Fictional Reality* highlights his dedication to supporting emerging writers and fostering creativity within the literary community.

From *Weekend Escape*'s unexpected plot twists to the atmospheric tension of *The Séance* and the historical realism of *The Leonids*, Paul's tales transport readers into worlds where the ordinary collides with the extraordinary. Endorsed by the legendary Shaun Hutson and applauded for his vivid storytelling and layered suspense, Paul J Jackson is a force to be reckoned with in the realm of horror and thriller fiction. It is our privilege to feature this exceptional author in this issue of *Reader's House*. Join us as we delve into Paul's creative process, inspirations, and expert advice for aspiring writers. Prepare to be enthralled!

What inspired you to write 'A New Life', and how did you develop its central theme of a couple's pact with an evil entity?

I guess the central theme for what the couple agree to do is grief. I know from experience that losing someone is utterly devastating and that you would do anything to see them again, to have them back. The offer of such a miracle is what drives the couple, even though they know it's wrong and will put someone else in danger. Coupled with guilt, their grief had made them selfish, had taken away their ability to think rationally, and had made them willing pawns in a sinister, twisted plan.

Where did the idea for the vengeful creature come from in 'Retribution' The Birth of a Horrifying Urban Legend, and how do you approach creating suspense and tension in your narratives?

The idea for it came from a short story I was writing for a competition. It was about an ancient yew tree growing in the middle of a cemetery and it was the ending I gave it that inspired me to write the novella. I liked the short story so much that I included it in the book to give the reader more context of the creature's origin.

With most of my stories the suspense and tension is usually introduced early on to grab the reader's attention and I strive to build on that throughout the book with each chapter adding more depth and detail.

I was thrilled to receive a 5-star review and gold award from Literary Titan for it, and even more so to be endorsed by Shaun Hutson, the godfather of gore. A writer I have admired for a long time.

> Paul J Jackson masterfully crafts engaging, spine-chilling stories with impactful characters, proving his remarkable skill in the horror genre.

How did Shaun Hutson come to endorse your work?

After being long-listed and short-listed in two competitions, as well as being published in their anthologies, I decided to run my own writing contest and created Pulp Fictional.com. Both my short story and flash fiction competitions were a great success and the quality of the work I received from around the world was outstanding. Having such talented new writers entering my contest I knew I needed a VIP judge to choose the top three stories from each to give them the prestige they deserved.

Cheekily, I approached Shaun Hutson who was delighted to be asked and agreed right away, much to my utter amazement. He not only chose the winning three stories from both contests, and wrote brief reviews for each, but he also sent me two of his own unpublished stories for the anthology I had planned. It was such an honour. He then later endorsed my work and sent me quotes to use on my books.

The anthology 'Fictional Reality' is the result of that competition for which I created the cover for, edited, and also have two stories in. Unfortunately, the contest had taken up way more of my time than expected and, being self employed, I struggled to continue and ended up shelving Pulp Fictional.com for the time being.

However, I am extremely proud of what we all achieved and believe 'Fictional Reality' is the best writing competition anthology out there today.

Your collection 'A Pound of Flash' features 50 stories, each under 1,000 words. What are the unique challenges and rewards of writing flash fiction compared to longer works?

Well, the first drafts of my flash fiction stories often exceed 1000 words and I find the main challenge then is to edit them down without ruining their structure or plot. I like stories to have a beginning, a middle, and a satisfying end, so the reward is getting all that to work in 1000 words or less. It certainly feels like an achievement when I end up with something I'm happy with.

With longer stories I can afford to include more detail and not worry about the word count as much. That said, I'm not keen on long chapters either, so I'm still mindful to some degree.

Just to let you know, I created the cover for 'A Pound of Flash' with a pack of steak and two, bloody livers that I cooked in a stir-fry after and ate.

'Weekend Escape' presents a plot where a planned murder in the woods takes an unexpected turn. What challenges do you encounter when writing plot twists, and how do you ensure they are both surprising and believable?

I think the best plot twists are the ones you don't see coming and the challenge is to hide them from the reader for as long as possible, or to decide when to reveal them that best suits the story without ruining the plot and losing the readers interest in it.

It can be tricky to get it right at times and I have found that the best way to keep my plot twists surprising is to have more than one if possible or to make sure the main story is gripping enough to prevent the reader from guessing the ending. Weekend Escape, for instance, keeps the reader focussed on Marcus as he is chased back to a cabin in the woods and hopefully prevents them from jumping to a conclusion too soon.

'Carbon Copy' features a wrongfully accused inmate seeking revenge. What research did you undertake to accurately portray the psychological aspects of your characters?

I try to base a lot of my character's psychological aspects on my own experiences, or those experienced by close family and friends. Fears, phobias, and unsettling situations tend to leave longer lasting psychological impressions on us all and I try include those in my stories. Claustrophobia for instance, or the fear of death, can trigger powerful emotions and this futuristic story contains both those elements.

Being a massive horror fan also helps with character observations, and I've probably seen them all, but real life experiences are much easier to relate to and easier to explain to the reader if you're familiar with the feeling you're describing.

'The Séance' introduces a terrifying demon targeting an unborn child. How do you balance supernatural elements with psychological horror in your stories?

> "Paul J Jackson delivers spine-chilling brilliance with *Down a Dark Path.* Each tale explores harrowing twists, sinister foes, and supernatural dread. Immersive storytelling, perfect for horror enthusiasts. Highly recommended for a thrilling escape!"

I think a fair balance between the two elements consists of a good description of the supernatural element, so that the reader understands the threat, coupled with the thoughts of those affected by it. We all know that horror fiction often depicts supernatural beings and situations that simply don't exist in the real world, but getting a good balance between both elements gives the reader a fuller picture and enables them to imagine the scene more clearly.

'The Leonids' involves a sinister plan during a meteor shower. How do you incorporate real-world events or phenomena into your fiction to enhance its realism?

I've always been a bit of a stargazer, thanks largely to walks at night with my father when I was a lad, and it was he who told me about several meteor showers that occur annually after we saw a shooting star. It turns out that every 33 years or so The Leonids shower intensifies into a meteor storm and I set the story during one that had been well documented in 1833. I liked the timeline of that, and the idea of mixing old and new concepts, and kept the realism of that time by describing items used back then, like flintlock pistols and oil lamps.

As an author known for your gripping tales, what advice would you offer to aspiring writers aiming to craft compelling horror and thriller narratives?

I would say, try to keep your characters as believable as possible and imagine yourself being in the situation you have put them in. Think how you would react in that situation, what you would do, or say, and how others around you would react. Realistic behaviour and dialogue in any fictional world you dream up, no matter how farfetched, encourages the reader to be more inclined to accept it and get drawn in.

From Fibromyalgia to Freedom: Healing and Empowerment

Shari Emami discusses her fibromyalgia journey, holistic healing methods, and her book Breaking Free From Pain, offering practical advice and emotional support for chronic pain sufferers.

SHARI EMAMI

SHARES HER JOURNEY OF HEALING AND HOLISTIC LIVING IN BREAKING FREE FROM PAIN

Editor's Desk I London

Shari Emami is a remarkable figure whose life and work embody resilience, compassion, and a deep commitment to holistic healing. An award-winning author, guest speaker, and published writer, Shari has transformed her personal struggles with fibromyalgia into a powerful platform for advocacy and education. As a board-certified holistic health practitioner and health coach, she has dedicated her life to exploring natural healing methods, ultimately achieving a pain-free life since 2016. Her journey is not just one of personal triumph but also a testament to the transformative power of holistic living.

Beyond her professional achievements, Shari is a passionate advocate for animal rights, volunteering with The Humane League and promoting a plant-based lifestyle. Her multifaceted approach to wellness—encompassing physical, emotional, and ethical dimensions—makes her a truly inspiring voice in the realms of health and literature.

In this exclusive interview for *Reader's House Magazine*, Shari opens up about her latest book, *Breaking Free From Pain*, a deeply personal and insightful guide that draws from her own experiences and extensive research in holistic medicine. She shares pivotal moments from her healing journey, practical advice for those battling fibromyalgia, and the emotional tools that have helped her and countless others reclaim their lives. For aspiring authors, Shari also offers invaluable advice on writing about personal health journeys, emphasising the therapeutic and transformative power of

"I wanted to share my viewpoint and what worked for me in terms of managing my pain."

sharing one's story.

Join us as we delve into the mind and heart of Shari Emami, a woman whose wisdom, empathy, and dedication continue to inspire and heal.

What inspired you to write "Breaking Free From Pain"?

I have always loved writing and during my trials and tribulations of trying to pinpoint what was causing my aches and pains, I was inspired to write my book. I figured through what I went through , the ups and downs and what I found to be helpful towards my own healing, gave me the courage to write my book. I was also heavily influenced by the teachings of Dr. Paul Eck and hair mineral analysis testing, as a non-invasive diagnostic tool. He is known as "the founding father" of hair mineral testing. It's an important testing technique to look at cellular activity in the system and mineral imbalances. It can reveal a lot about your health. In addition, through my own journey and battle, I wanted to share my viewpoint and what worked for me in terms of managing my pain. Through my studies, I also wanted to share my knowledge in holistic medicine and healing modalities. My book goes into a lot of details on methods the readers can use to help with their treatment plan.

Shari Emami's wisdom and compassion shine through her work, inspiring countless individuals to embrace holistic healing and reclaim their lives from chronic pain.

Can you share a pivotal moment in your journey with fibromyalgia that influenced your healing process?

I wanted to understand the mind and body connection. I started to understand how through working with various doctors and naturopaths that there was both a physical and emotional aspect to getting fibromyalgia.

How do you approach the emotional aspects of living with fibromyalgia in your book?

In my book, I talk about various therapy techniques and offer interactive journals and exercises that can help, and have been backed up by research . I also talk about trauma and chronic stress as being a major component to getting fibromyalgia. Chapter 3 is a bit personal, but it is essential to my story as it gives readers lessons to learn from toxic relationships and how they can harm your mental and physical health. There is a good chapter on how to handle the emotional challenges of dealing with pain and who to reach out to, how to get help.

What practical advice do you offer to those currently struggling with fibromyalgia?

It takes a good team of doctors, and natural healers to come up with ways to cope and figure out how to lessen the pain. I have several techniques written in my book and a list of what types of alternative therapy treatments can do for you. This includes massage therapy, acupuncture , chiropractic care and much more. There is also information on what type of therapists to go to and community support.

How do you incorporate holistic healing modalities into your daily routine?

I'm a holistic health practitioner and health coach and I always start the day with meditation, good nutrition and a light workout. I want to make sure I'm properly fueled and get a good workout routine, but one that is more low impact.

What role do you believe community support plays in managing chronic pain conditions like fibromyalgia?

There are so many religious and emotional support groups to reach out to. It's important to meet others that share similar struggles that you are dealing with. There you can gain some great coping tools on dealing with chronic pain. You may make some friends too!

What advice would you give to aspiring authors who wish to write about their personal health journeys?

I would say don't hold back. Carve out time each day or every other day to write and say what you want to say. Start with your concept , message and outline and then go from there. It's so therapeutic and when your message gets across to others and can help them, it's the best feeling ever.

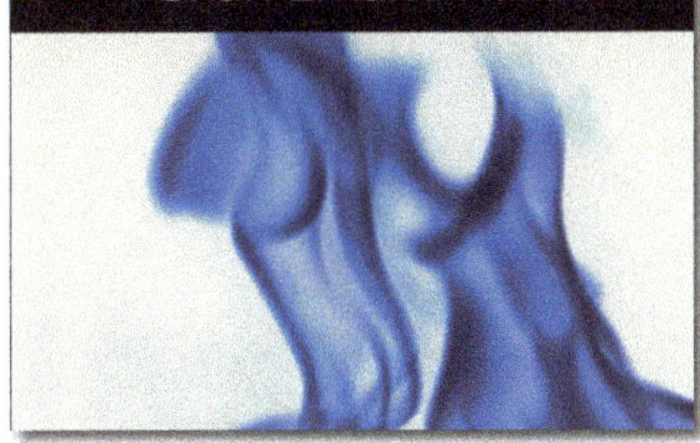

Shari Emami's *Breaking Free From Pain* is a heartfelt memoir and guide on overcoming fibromyalgia. Blending personal experience with practical healing strategies, she offers hope, resilience, and holistic approaches to managing pain. This empowering book is essential for fibromyalgia sufferers, their loved ones, and healthcare professionals seeking deeper understanding.

PHOTO:*Sheryl C.D. Ickes, award-winning author, draws inspiration from her life as a lorry driver and cake decorator to craft captivating mysteries.*

Mysteries With Heart, Humour, And Authenticity

SHERYL C.D. ICKES

WEAVES LIFE'S PASSIONS INTO CAPTIVATING COSY MYSTERIES

Mitzi Perdue shares strategies for sustaining family businesses across generations, emphasizing endowed vacations, stewardship, philanthropy, and managing family quarrels to maintain strong family culture and business longevity.

AS TOLD TO BEN ALAN

"My stories are a celebration of everyday professions and the extraordinary people behind them." - Ickes

Sheryl C.D. Ickes is a master of turning life's unique experiences into captivating cozy mysteries. An award-winning author, Sheryl draws from her rich background as a cross-country truck driver and cake decorator to craft stories that are as authentic as they are imaginative. Her debut novel, *Death of a Dispatcher*, introduces readers to Becky Bridgewater, a trucker-turned-sleuth navigating the open road and unraveling mysteries in a profession rarely explored in fiction. With a perfect blend of suspense and charm, Sheryl's work offers a fresh perspective on both trucking and storytelling.

Equally delightful is her "Slice of Life Mysteries" series, where cake decorating takes a sinister turn in the small town of Creek Water, Pennsylvania. Titles like *It Only Takes One Bite* showcase her talent for balancing humor, suspense, and unforgettable characters. Whether she's writing about the open highways or the secrets of small-town bakeries, Sheryl's stories are infused with authenticity, wit, and heart.

With multiple series under her belt, including ventures into children's literature, Sheryl C.D. Ickes has carved a unique niche in the literary world. Her books are not just mysteries—they're celebrations of life's quirks, the beauty of everyday professions, and the joy of a well-told story.

Death of a Dispatcher, like many in the world of cozies, introduces a fun mystery set within a small-town. What inspired you to create the character of Becky

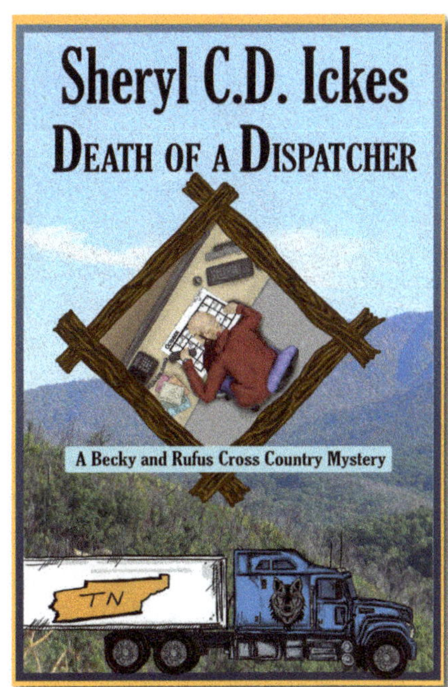

'Death of a Dispatcher' by Sheryl C.D. Ickes is a captivating cozy mystery set in the unique world of cross-country trucking. Becky and Rufus are a lovable duo, and the plot is filled with suspense, twists, and heartfelt moments. A fresh, engaging debut that leaves readers eager for more adventures!

Bridgewater, and how did you pick her unique profession of being a cross-country truck driver?

I grew up with a love of trucking. My dad was an owner operator (someone who owns the truck he also drives) and a mechanic. He taught me to drive truck because I asked him to after years of going along with him on his different trips whenever possible. I also like to drive and to travel. Dad was a local driver, basically delivering and picking up in any state that bordered Pennsylvania and a few beyond, making it possible to be home every night. Years ago, my husband and I were a cross-country truck driving team. Since only one person can drive at a time, if I wasn't sleeping or checking out the scenery, I would read. Cozy murder mysteries are my favorite genre. I felt that trucking and cozies could be blended together nicely. This way one could avoid killing off half of a small town as the series continues and I could introduce people to some wonderful truck drivers and different states and small towns. I haven't read nor found any cozies with this profession, so I believe it's rather unique.

Sheryl C.D. Ickes masterfully creates heartfelt, authentic mysteries, blending humour and suspense with unique professions and unforgettable characters.

The balance between suspense and character development is crucial when building a compelling mystery read. How do you approach the concept of establishing depth within your cast of characters, while trying not to overburden the novel from too much backstory?

I like to write similar to how I like to read, meaning not a lot of details upon details upon details. Once I write a story, I reread it looking for a multitude of different issues; one of which is if I provided enough character development without too much. I want readers to understand who each character is without becoming bored, hopefully I strike the correct balance.

Small towns often have a charm and secrecy about them, which plays a role in Death of a Dispatcher. How does the setting of Tennessee add to the atmosphere of your story, and how does it differentiate from any upcoming installments in the series?

No two states in the United States of America are the same, each having its own charms and issues. Tennessee is a wonderful state with gorgeous scenery, rich history, and great people. Southern USA is also very different from the North in numerous ways: food, speed of life, humor, and folklore to name a few. I try to draw from each state's assets as I write and incorporate its differences. Each of my books will be placed in a different state and follow the journey of my cross-country trucking team of Becky and Rufus Bridgewater.

Each author has their own process in developing their mysteries. Whether it be through pasting notecards in order, writing out an outline, or filing small scraps of ideas into a folder for a later time, no two authors give the exact same answer. Can you share with us a little bit of how you organize your notes into an engaging novel full of twists and turns?

I begin with an idea swirling in my head and a mental running of the storyline until I find a viable, plausible story. I may, or may not, write a few notes before just sitting down, and starting a mystery story, usually on my laptop. Once I've started, if I have numerous storylines running concurrently throughout a novel, I will use a day-to-day timeline to lay out the different storylines so that no one event occurs before it realistically should. Family and work have a tendency to slow down my progress, which I am definitely okay with, but the story keeps intruding in my thoughts. Therefore, when any kind of idea comes to mind, I write it down so I don't forget it. When I get back to my computer, I sometimes chuckle at the pile of napkins, receipts, scraps of paper, and backs of envelopes I have collected. I write what I know and experience, so anything I see, hear, smell, and even taste could end up in a book. Since one cannot always write depending on the activity, I also record voice memos on my cell phone, so that would also be considered part of the "note pile" when I get back to the computer. My way may not be for everyone, and is definitely a bit messy, but I believe it works for me and hopefully readers like the end result.

As an author, what do you hope readers take away from Death of a Dispatcher, and is there anything you would like them to know before diving into your story?

I know that there are quite a few misconceptions about trucking and truck drivers. I would like readers to enjoy my stories, and maybe see trucking from a different perspective. There are some great people out on the roads driving every day, and for many different reasons. I will also be honest, and state there is that small percentage, as in all professions, that can ruin it for the majority. Trucking can be fun, but it also has its share of danger. I believe that my stories based on my experience, and that of my husband and friends, can add some insight into trucking, while my imagination in creating the murder mystery part of my stories can combine to hopefully make an enjoyable read for all.

Exploring Women's Perspectives Through Fiction

Stella Atrium weaves powerful storytelling with thoughtful world-building, focusing on authentic female voices, real-world issues, and creating speculative fiction that merges political, social, and emotional depth.

STELLA ATRIUM

BRINGS REAL-WORLD DEPTH AND DIVERSE VOICES TO SPECULATIVE FICTION

Editot's Desk I London

"Big stories require investment—not just time, but understanding genuine human experiences."

Stella Atrium stands as a beacon of contemporary speculative fiction, her narratives both imaginative and deeply resonant with real-world themes. With a focus on genuine human experience and a dedication to showcasing the untold stories of women, she has carved a unique space within a genre often dominated by recurring archetypes. Most recently celebrated for her *Tribal Wars* series, Atrium transports readers to Dolvia, a richly textured world beyond the wormhole, rendering it with such evocative detail that it lingers long after the final page.

Atrium's work has always been marked by her sharp observation of the human condition and her commitment to exploring layered identities. From *The Bush Clinic,* which examines the resilience of women in conflict zones, to *The Body Politic*, where political courage intertwines with personal sacrifice, Atrium crafts narratives that challenge as much as they entertain. In *Seven Beyond*, she ventures into visionary and metaphysical territory, illustrating her versatility and literary breadth. Across her works, her female protagonists transcend the familiar princess-and-queen trope, emerging as ranchers, teachers, warriors, and diplomats, each steeped in authenticity.

Beyond her writing, Stella Atrium brings a wealth of scholarship to her craft. Having spent over two decades as a university instructor and creator of a course on migration flows, she infuses her stories with the richness of political, cultural, and social undercurrents. This ability to weave intricate societal structures and create compellingly human characters is what makes her speculative fiction not only immersive, but also profoundly relevant.

It is a privilege to share our conversation with such a celebrated author in this issue of *Reader's House*. Atrium's insights into storytelling, the responsibilities of a writer, and the delicate art of world-building promise to inspire seasoned authors and emerging writers alike. Stella Atrium continues to remind us all of the power of fiction in reflecting truths, challenging perceptions, and fostering understanding across boundaries—both earthly and intergalactic.

What inspired you to create female protagonists in your science fiction novels, and how do you believe their perspectives enrich the genre?

When I started THE TRIBAL WARS series – all those decades ago – I was looking at how women can thrive in a crisis zone. The men are off fighting in the militia. The women have no weapons, no education, no access to capital, no voice in the public square. Do they band together to protect the children, or do they undercut each other?

For the genre, my effort was to break out of the princess-or-evil-queen mold. I wanted to show women in all roles like street kids, ranchers, teachers, doctors, warriors, militia commanders, diplomats. How do they solve real world problems using the tools that women have? And I gave them a little magic for spice.

Male characters are not neglected, of course. We meet warriors, peace-keeping generals, underhanded businessmen, and a crusading journalist. My idea was that a woman is more interesting when an interesting man is interested in her.

In *The Bush Clinic*, you explore the challenges faced by women in conflict zones. Could you elaborate on the real-world issues that influenced this narrative?

The stories take place on a small mining planet but reflect some situations in today's world. The tribes must band together to create a strong duchy to stand up to offworld corporations that want to take the planet's mineral wealth. The tribal women quickly learn that they must first dislodge corrupt local officials.

For politics in a conflict zone, we must follow the money. Who is using peace-keeping funds to provide medical care or education for the tribal kids? Who is courting the invasive corporations to line their own pockets? Funds earmarked for altruistic goals seldom reach the intended stressed population. It's all talk and graft.

Stella Atrium masterfully combines authenticity, imagination, and social relevance, offering fresh perspectives and groundbreaking narratives in speculative fiction.

If we can expose this supply-line graft through works of fiction, perhaps we can shine a light on the practical outcomes of no accountability by looking at street level examples.

The Body Politic delves into political and personal dilemmas. How do you balance complex political themes with character development in your writing?

We learn about the needs and cares of several tribal women from the first story. In THE BODY POLITIC, these characters face a corrupt local official who wants to silence their protests.

Each woman in turn chooses death-by-fire in the public square, a painful way to die. Do not try this at home. This extreme form of protest is taken from real world situations across many conflicts. My first experience was a news report from the Vietnam war when a Buddhist monk used immolation to protest the American presence in his country.

One protestor is Mandy, the set-aside wife of the corrupt leader Rabbenu Ely. Her death-by-fire is defined by the offworld media as pitiful and desperate rather than a hard but righteous choice made to dramatize an unsafe situation. When the next admired women take this step, and the next, the ground begins to shift under Ely's rule.

Your *Tribal Wars* series is set on the planet Dolvia. What unique aspects of Dolvia's culture and environment do you find most compelling to write about?

One question I asked myself was how to maintain culture and give hope to the children in times of conflict? The tribes have a shared oral history with tales of great heroes, reinforced by campfire chants lauding today's warriors.

The composers of chants had unique voices, some like chronicles and some like ditties that were memorable for the rhyme. The old tales were each different due to the composers' styles. The challenge for me was to develop these voices that come out of the past with cautionary tales that had a small moral tacked onto the end. Great fun!

Seven Beyond is described as a visionary and metaphysical saga. How does this work differ from your previous novels in terms of themes and narrative style?

SEVEN BEYOND is a standalone novel written in a starkly different style. I think of it as my magnum opus, and I enjoy talking about the characters.

Christopher Meenins is an offworld scholar from a race that live 1000 years called Longists. At age 800 he has forgotten his past eras and believes that he's one of us, except he has bad dreams that are really his memory turning. The Longists send a companion named Linda Deemer to help Dr. Meenins accept his past guilty acts that changed race history.

This is a journey story where Christopher must discover the blue mountains of flint, the new colony restingplace, before he dies. They come out of Russia through the Caucasus, into the Middle East, across the Mediterranean, around Spain to London, England where they catch a ride on the Concorde to NYC. Traveling companions come and go, and Linda Deemer relates tales of race history from another galaxy until they reach the flinty mountains and Dr. Meenins can find his rest.

The story talks about accepting the consequences of guilty acts, finding redemption, group loyalty, and how we define ourselves based on shared stories.

As a seasoned author, how do you approach world-building to ensure that your speculative fiction settings feel both immersive and believable?

Ah, there are many writer tools. One technique is placing the character in her daily complaints such as wet shoes or cold coffee. Report the sensory detail to anchor the reader in the scene. What smells, tastes, sounds, sources of light – and these are imbued with the character's fears, needs, reaction to interruption and more.

Developing unique voices demands that the writer knows the characters well, spending time with them as more than agents of the plot. I tend to meander around with their personal concerns until the story has grown to 160,000 words. I had to learn to cut the delicious personal moments, to sacrifice some of my best writing for the sake of word count. LOL

I kept loyal to my writerly challenge to show how real women respond to real crises. Characters are conflicted, selfish, and maybe even cowardly. Acts of heroism are seldom, whereas questions of identity and one's place within the group are many.

Stella Atrium's The Matrix Opal is an immersive fantasy debut filled with political intrigue, layered characters, and poetic themes of truth and integrity. With rich world-building, moral complexity, and a philosophical edge, this standalone addition to The Duchy Wars series captivates readers who enjoy nuanced storytelling and elevated speculative fiction.

Your novels often feature characters navigating complex societal structures. How do you ensure that these structures are both intricate and accessible to readers?

I'm glad you asked that question. Action adventure is about the hero who has an unrelenting pursuit of a single goal, and all others must get behind him in the journey over obstacles that leads to triumph and acclaim. Except life doesn't work that way. Mostly, we accommodate ourselves to solving problems in a larger situation like buying groceries when eggs cost $9 a dozen. There's drama in everyday life, hard choices that come from dissatisfaction and loyalty to others who are suffering the same indignities.

The hero may win the day, but the political situation is unchanged. By shining a light on some real-world problems that never make the news, I hope to bring a fresh understanding to how we can bring real help to neglected groups.

What advice would you offer to aspiring authors looking to write speculative fiction that authentically represents diverse female experiences?

Count the cost – especially for time invested in developing big stories. New writers often believe in their voices and their complaints, but are not thinking about the consequences of spending endless hours alone in a dimly lit room with characters only you know while your real-life loved ones are getting on with it.

Keep it real – especially for female characters who are more than their outrage at the powers-that-be. How do we address the immediate problem? What unique solutions are ours that come from experience and scholarship?

Show the darker emotions – leave behind the princess mentality and dig into insecurities, anger, resentment, a need for vengeance. Women have all of these. The motif of a privileged princess raised in ignorance and with no weapons training no longer works.

From China to Canada, A Literary Journey Rooted in Memory and Resilience

Tong Ge shares the inspiration behind The House Filler, explores cultural identity, discusses writing across languages, and offers heartfelt advice to aspiring authors crafting historical fiction with authenticity and purpose.

TONG GE

REFLECTS ON HERITAGE, HISTORY, AND THE POWER OF STORYTELLING IN HER ACCLAIMED DEBUT THE HOUSE FILLER

by Z. Roberts I London

"Strong protagonists who face overwhelming odds inspire readers, reminding them of their own strength and resilience."

Tong Ge stands as a remarkable figure in the literary world, with a journey that traces from the bustling landscapes of China to the vast prairies of Canada. Armed with a Master of Science degree from the University of Saskatchewan, she embarked on a literary career that beautifully melds her deep-rooted Chinese heritage with the creative freedoms of her adopted homeland. Since 2012, she has captivated audiences with her poetry, prose, and short stories written in both English and Chinese, with her works reaching readers across North America, England, and Taiwan.

Her debut novel, "The House Filler," is a testament to her storytelling prowess, weaving a narrative that spans decades of Chinese history, and it has earned her numerous accolades including the 2024 Independent Press Award for new fiction. This poignant exploration of resilience in the face of systemic oppression, inspired by her grandmother's story, resonates deeply with readers, as evidenced by its status as a finalist for prestigious awards like the Eyelands Book Awards and Canadian Book Club Awards.

Tong Ge's ability to navigate the intricacies of writing in two languages enriches her storytelling, imbuing her work with a unique cultural authenticity. Her craftsmanship is evident in her meticulous research, ensuring historical accuracy while maintaining an engaging narrative - a skill honed through her personal experiences and the vibrant multicultural environment of Canada. This, coupled with a keen sense of historical context and cultural sensitivity, elevates her narratives to a point where they not only reflect past realities but also challenge readers to reflect on contemporary issues.

For aspiring authors, particularly those navigating the complex paths of historical fiction or cultural narratives, Tong Ge serves as an inspiring guide. Her dedication to authenticity, cultural sensitivity, and her commitment to crafting original, heartfelt stories offer invaluable lessons. Her works not only shed light on historical truths but also celebrate the enduring strength of the human spirit, reminding us all of the persistent hope and resilience that define our shared humanity.

What inspired you to write The House Filler, and how did you develop its central themes?

My grandmother's story inspired The House Filler, which explores a woman's resilience against systemic oppression and personal adversity, with themes of love, sacrifice and survival across generations. Drawing from my grandmother's experiences and my knowledge of Chinese history, this theme evolved naturally.

How has your personal experience of moving from China to Canada shaped your storytelling and perspectives as a writer?

Canada's freedom has allowed me to write without fear or self-censorship, something I couldn't do in China. Here, I also learned the craft of creative writing, as China only began offering formal creative writing programs in 2004. I'm grateful for Canada's supportive writing environment, including critique groups, beta readers, freelance editors, and the invaluable library system. Over the years, I've borrowed countless books, which has helped me grow into an award-winning author and given me the confidence to continue creating meaningful work.

> Tong Ge is a gifted writer whose lyrical prose, cultural insight, and emotional depth captivate readers across languages and literary traditions.

The House Filler spans multiple decades of Chinese history—what challenges did you face in ensuring historical accuracy while keeping the narrative engaging?

Historical accuracy is a challenge for all writers of historical fiction. For me, it's less of a compromise, as I grew up in China, reading in Chinese and listening to family stories. These became the foundation for my book. In 2015, I visited my grandmother's hometown and met relatives, which brought the setting to life. The internet made research easier, providing books, newspapers from the 1930s and 1940s, and historical photos that helped me accurately depict the settings. To keep the narrative engaging, I focused on plot, pacing, conflict, emotional depth, and vivid details, which aligned with historical truth. Though I've spent many years honing my craft, I continue to improve with each book.

Your novel has received multiple awards and nominations. What do you believe makes it resonate so strongly with readers?

The book's originality, unique voice and distinctive setting, along with vivid depictions of culture, history and social environment, resonate with readers. Additionally, strong protagonists who face overwhelming odds, struggle, and find solace and hope inspire readers, reminding them of their own strength and resilience.

You have written and published in both English and Chinese. How does writing in different languages influence your creative process and storytelling approach?

Writing fiction in a second language is both a blessing and a curse. The blessing is using Chinese sayings and proverbs to add authenticity, but the differences between Chinese and English present challenges. For example, Chinese only has one tense (the present), lacks plurals, and doesn't change verbs with the subject. Prepositions are also used differently. After over 30 years in Canada, I've become more familiar with English expressions, but I must be cautious about incorporating them into my novels set in China, as they don't always fit the cultural context.

Can you share insights into your writing routine? Do you have any particular rituals or habits that help you stay focused?

Since 2005, my commission-based job has allowed flexible hours. For the first 15 years, I worked from 9 a.m. to 9 p.m., then dedicated two to four hours to writing, which I call my "happy hour." I don't have rituals and often lose track of time once I start. The key for me is quiet—peace and calm help me stay focused.

What key messages or emotions do you hope readers take away from The House Filler?

The struggles of early 20th-century China—wars, totalitarian regimes, poverty, class and gender inequality—remain relevant today. Freedom is fragile and can be lost in an instant if we're not vigilant. I want readers to reflect on whether humans are inherently cruel, or if war turns us into beasts. I believe, without consequences, humans can commit atrocities. While some may feel sadness reading the book, I hope they are also inspired by the resilience of the human spirit and recognize that as long as we are alive, there is hope.

What advice would you give to aspiring authors, particularly those looking to write historical fiction or stories that bridge different cultures?

My advice is to stay true to your story and voice. Don't follow trends—your subject will already make your work unique. Research is essential, especially if you're unfamiliar with the period or language. However, research as you write and revise, rather than doing it all upfront. If possible, visit the settings of your novel.

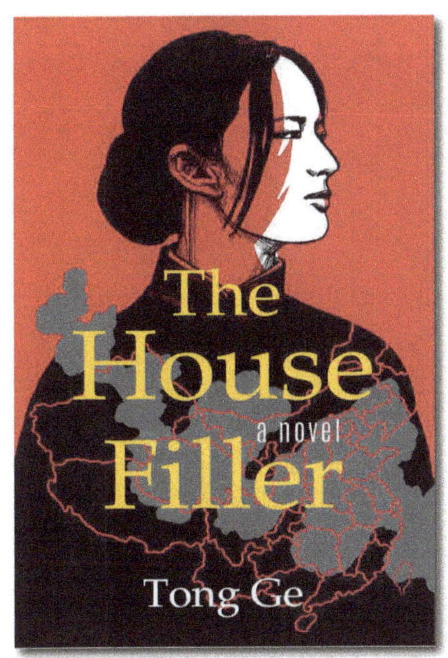

> *The House Filler* follows Golden Phoenix, a widow navigating war-torn 20th-century China. Amidst famine, political oppression, and Japanese occupation, she fights to keep her family together. Separated from her children and enduring immense suffering, her story is one of resilience and maternal strength, ending as the Cultural Revolution looms.

When researching, read books from the period, especially fiction, for richer, more authentic details. Once your manuscript is done, have someone familiar with the culture and history review it, ideally someone who speaks the language. This could even be a friend, not necessarily a professional consultant. Many mistakes arise when second-generation immigrants unknowingly insert inaccuracies, and consulting a first-generation person could help avoid this.

Even a renowned writer like Pearl S. Buck made such mistakes in her book Imperial Woman, which contains historical inaccuracies about Empress Dowager Cixi. Her failure to consult Chinese experts led to errors, including a misrepresented book cover for the audiobook published in 2011. Today, sensitivity consultants are key for cultural authenticity, and publishers should consult them, especially for unfamiliar cultures.

Also, avoid projecting modern norms into historical fiction. For example, some recent novels inaccurately portray teenage rebellion, which wasn't typical in past generations. Be mindful of historical context when portraying social dynamics.

Finally, be open to feedback. If multiple people highlight the same issue, it's time to reconsider it.

A Conversation with the Author of Freeze Frame and Med Hunters

Tyler Beauchamp discusses his journey as a paediatrician and bestselling author, exploring mental health, creative writing, and his new series.

TYLER BEAUCHAMP

HIS JOURNEY FROM PAEDIATRICS TO BESTSELLER AUTHOR

Editot's Desk I London

"During the pandemic, I saw so many kids and adolescents struggling with their mental health, isolated during a time in their lives designed for interaction. Stories connect us in ways we can't ever imagine. They lift us up, and they bring us together."

Tyler Beauchamp stands as a remarkable beacon of creativity and compassion in today's literary landscape. As a Pediatric Resident and Children's/YA Author hailing from Georgia, Ty's dual commitment to medicine and storytelling reflects a profound understanding of the complexities of youth. Graduating from The University of North Carolina, he has seamlessly intertwined his passions, producing works that not only entertain but also resonate deeply with the experiences of young readers. His debut novel, *Freeze Frame*, quickly ascended to the pinnacle of success, becoming an Amazon #1 Bestseller in Coming-of-Age fiction, while its forthcoming television adaptation signals a bright future for his captivating narrative.

In this exclusive interview, we delve into the heart of Beauchamp's creative process, exploring the rich themes of identity, trauma, and the profound impact of mental health. His insights reveal not just the narrative choices behind *Freeze Frame* but also the inspiration drawn from his experiences during the pandemic, where he witnessed firsthand the struggles faced by adolescents. This desire to connect, uplift, and heal is evident throughout his work, as he masterfully crafts stories that encourage young adults to seek help and share their burdens.

Beauchamp's upcoming series, *Med Hunters: Rage of the Rhino*, promises to take readers on an exhilarating journey, blending the realms of medicine and fantasy in a way that is both imaginative and accessible. As he balances the demanding roles of physician and author, his dedication to fostering the well-being of his patients while captivating the hearts of his readers is nothing short of inspiring.

Join us as we explore the world of Tyler Beauchamp—a storyteller whose unique voice adds a vital layer to the discourse on mental health, resilience, and the transformative power of narrative. His journey from independent filmmaking to becoming a bestselling author serves as a testament to the healing capacity of stories, reminding us that, ultimately, literature holds the power to connect us all.

How has your medical background influenced the themes and character development in your novel *"Freeze Frame"*?

While this story isn't about medicine, so to speak, it touches on themes that are pervasive in adolescent medicine: loss of identity, self-harm and suicidality, trauma and PTSD. I wanted to tell a story to help young adults struggling and help them feel heard. Freeze Frame was made to highlight how everyone lives out their own trauma uniquely and to encourage us all to ask for help when we need it.

"*Freeze Frame*" addresses issues such as childhood trauma, PTSD, and mental health. What inspired you to explore these particular topics in your writing?

During the pandemic, I saw so many kids and adolescents struggling with their mental health, isolated during a time in their lives designed for interaction. In the hospital or in clinic, you hear so many of them express concerns of being alone. All you want to do is open every door, have them step out in the hall, and see they are anything but alone. That's where stories can go where medicine can't. Stories connect us in ways we can't ever imagine. They lift us up, and they bring us together.

The protagonist in "*Freeze Frame*" grapples with an ever-changing reality. Could you elaborate on the significance of this narrative choice and its intended impact on readers?

I think it's brutal the amount of pressure the world places on teens today. They simultaneously are told they're too young and don't understand enough while also being told they have to be perfect to have a good future. It's no wonder rates of anxiety and depression have never been higher. I wanted my protagonist to exemplify that internal struggle, and more importantly, how to find the road to healing.

A heartfelt exploration of adolescent struggles, blending medical insight and powerful storytelling.

Your upcoming series, "*Med Hunters: Rage of the Rhino,*" features twins with superhuman abilities combating fantastical monsters. What can readers expect from this new venture, and how does it differ from your previous work?

Get ready, because Med Hunters is heading in an entirely new direction! Rage of the Rhino, the first book in my new series, will take young readers on an exciting sci-fi adventure that brings the world of medicine to life. After an experiment gone wrong turns diseases into fantasy monsters, the town of Marshboro is under attack. Luckily, twins Beck and Timmy Lewis are here to save the day. With the help of a friendly, mad scientist, Beck and Timmy must master their newfound bio-powers to hunt down these medical monsters before everyone falls untreatably ill.

Balancing a career in paediatrics with writing must present challenges. How do you manage your time between these two demanding professions?

Honestly, the answer isn't sexy. The old adage "You make time for the things you love" holds true. The counterintuitive secret is that when you make time for the things that fill you with life and joy, you find time for everything else. The beauty about writing is that 99% of it isn't putting words to page. Most of writing is thinking about your stories, picturing your characters, feeling your themes. No matter how busy life gets, there is always time to take a moment to close your eyes and think. The more you practice that, the more you find time to put those thoughts on the page.

"Freeze Frame" has been adapted into a television series currently being pitched to streaming services. Can you share any insights into this adaptation process and what viewers might anticipate?

The process has been a dream come true. Over the last few years, we've adapted the story into a limited series, filmed a proof-of-concept pilot, and are currently pitching the series! I've caught myself crying only a few hundred times seeing my characters come to life and picturing the idea of spreading this story to an even wider audience. I think both readers of "Freeze Frame" and newcomers are going to fall in love with what is heading their way.

Your journey from independent filmmaking in Savannah to becoming a published author and paediatrician is remarkable. How have these diverse experiences shaped your storytelling approach?

I really started writing as a kid because of my chronic pain, spending so much time in waiting rooms or just in a bad mental state, I needed an escape. I never thought that my life would end up revolving around writing and medicine years later. Having a foot in two wildly separate worlds, I hope to bring them together in a way that hasn't been done to truly serve kids and young adults. Medicine allow us to do miraculous things and sustain life, stories allow us to sustain our soul. I hope my experience in medicine will not only help me protect my patients' hearts, but I intend to keep writing stories to help my patients and others like them feel heard.

What advice would you offer to aspiring authors, especially those balancing writing with other professional commitments?

Biggest advice for writing: Start. Right now. Don't wait for the right class, mentor, or moment. Start getting words on the page as soon as you can, and don't be afraid to throw away 90% of what you write. You'll find sometimes, after hours of writing; you might only have a sentence or two you really like. But if that's what it took to get that little piece of gold, it was worth it. Second, you'll find a lot of advice on "finding your process," and I promise all of it comes down to trial and error. There isn't a formula, and you'll be told everything that worked for other people: it doesn't mean it's for you. Take it all with a grain of salt. If what you're doing isn't working, try something new, but trust your process. If you really want to write, part of you has to treat it like a job...especially if you have another job. Carve out a said time for it every day or every week, and absolutely protect that time. Even if you don't get a single usable word out of it, you spent that time finding what you didn't want to include. That's just as important. Lastly, never forget you are meant to make people feel something. A good story wraps you into a new world and captivates you in ways you never expect. At the end, you feel relieved, sad, angry, or jubilated. But you feel. It's a blessing to make people feel; never forget that.

Freeze Frame by Tyler Beauchamp is a captivating debut that intricately weaves the struggles of a troubled teen filmmaker. With its dynamic portrayal of friendship and the battle against one's past, the narrative is both poignant and engaging. Beauchamp's masterful storytelling makes for a compelling read that resonates deeply. Highly recommended!

NAVIGATING GRIEF THROUGH CHILDREN'S EYES

Y.Y. Chan shares her journey of transforming personal grief into children's literature, emphasizing the importance of addressing difficult topics and using writing as a therapeutic tool for healing and understanding.

Y.Y. CHAN

Y.Y. CHAN DISCUSSES THE IMPORTANCE OF ADDRESSING DIFFICULT TOPICS IN CHILDREN'S BOOKS

EDITOR'S DESK

Y.Y. Chan is a remarkable voice in contemporary children's literature, hailing from Hong Kong and captivating readers worldwide with her poignant storytelling. Her works are celebrated for their emotional depth and courage in addressing complex themes such as grief and loss, making her a multi-award-winning author. Chan's ability to weave narratives that resonate with both young and adult audiences is a testament to her skill and sensitivity as a writer. Her books, including the acclaimed "Can You Hear Me, Daddy?" and "Grandma, It's Me!", are not just stories but essential tools that help families and educators navigate difficult conversations with children. Through her writing, Chan offers solace and understanding, encouraging readers to embrace their emotions and find hope amidst life's challenges.

In this insightful interview with Reader's House Magazine, Y.Y. Chan shares her journey as an author and educator, revealing the personal experiences that have shaped her narratives. Her passion for storytelling is evident as she discusses the importance of addressing societal issues through children's literature and the therapeutic power of writing. Chan's dedication to fostering empathy and emotional intelligence in young readers is truly inspiring, and her works continue to leave a lasting impact on families and communities around the world.

Y.Y. Chan, celebrated author, shares her passion for storytelling and her journey of transforming personal experiences into impactful children's literature.

Your debut picture book, Can You Hear Me, Daddy?, tackles the complex and emotional topic of grief through the eyes of a child. How did your personal experience of losing your father shape the narrative, and what message do you hope young readers will take away from Renee's story?

My experience of losing my father to cancer at first inspired me to write a memoir. As I began, I realized I couldn't remember some details clearly and didn't want to share some details with others, so I reframed it into a story for children. I wrote from the perspective of a

"Celebrating Mid-Autumn Festival" by Eugenia Chu is a delightful introduction to one of Asia's most cherished holidays. With engaging storytelling and beautiful illustrations, it brings history, traditions, and joyful activities to life for young readers.

young girl rather than an adult. The events are fictional, but the emotions are real. I considered how I would have felt losing my father as a child, imagining conversations I would have wanted with him—what I wanted to say and what I wished he could have said to me. The message I hope readers take away is that, while loss is inevitable, our loved ones remain in our hearts. We can keep talking to them whenever we want. It's normal to grieve and feel sad; we only grieve because we love.

In both Can You Hear Me, Daddy? and Grandma, It's Me!, you address difficult subjects like death and dementia in a way that is accessible to children. What inspired you to write about these topics, and how do you approach making such heavy themes relatable for young audiences?

Growing up in an Asian family, I often felt that topics like death should not be discussed. It is considered unlucky to talk about it, and some even keep terminal diagnoses secret from their family members. Ignoring these realities only causes more harm and suffering. In the final moments, we can't avoid the topic, leading to difficulty coping and sometimes regret. Many think children are too young to understand, but they are very aware of death and illness. While starting these conversations can be tough, they are essential for helping children understand the world and express their emotions during these events. I wish I had read more books on this topic when I was a child, as they could have helped me cope better as an adult. We must be realistic and age-appropriate without being graphic when writing about these topics for children. The key is to include genuine emotions, as readers may not relate to specific scenarios but can connect with a character's feelings and thoughts.

Y.Y. Chan is a masterful storyteller, skilfully addressing complex emotions and fostering empathy in young readers through her heartfelt narratives.

Journaling plays a significant role in your stories, serving as a tool for your characters to process their emotions. Why do you believe journaling is an important practice for children, especially when dealing with grief and loss?

It can be difficult to express our emotions to family and friends verbally. And sometimes, we are not ready to talk about them with others. Yet, we need an outlet to express them. Writing has often been therapeutic for me. It doesn't need to be shared so it doesn't need to be perfect or grammatically correct. It's simply a personal and private collection of your experiences and emotions. Journaling is a way for everyone to process their emotions without fear of judgement, and it also becomes a keepsake of all your memories and experiences with your loved ones. This practice allows us to process our emotions by identifying what they are, why we feel that way and possibly reveal any insights, epiphanies or action steps to move forward. For those who may not have the skills to write or are too young to form coherent sentences, they can draw or record audio or video clips instead. It's simply a record of your experiences and feelings. You may choose to share them with others later or keep them private.

Your books have received high praise for their ability to foster conversations about loss and memory in families, schools, and communities. What feedback have you received from readers, particularly from parents and educators, regarding the impact of your books?

Many parents have shared that after reading these stories with their children, they became more open about difficult topics and more attuned to their family and friends' feelings. With Grandma, It's Me! which is about dementia, the story helped children be more patient and understanding toward their grandparents and other elderly people. Families with members suffering from dementia found ways to connect and communicate more effectively, strengthening their bonds. I also used this book to teach my students, which sparked conversations about caring for the elderly and some students also shared their experiences with grandparents who had other illnesses. For Can You Hear Me, Daddy?, parents mentioned that the story brought them hope and peace. Despite its sadness, the ending reassures them that their loved ones will always be remembered and loved. This book was used in a Hong Kong kindergarten, where children drew pictures before, during, and after listening to the story. Many drawings reflected a shift in perspective, moving from sadness and darkness to joy and hope.

As an award-winning author, how do you view the role of children's literature in addressing societal issues and personal challenges? How do you ensure your stories are both comforting and educational for young readers?

Children's literature is vital in shaping the values, morals, and beliefs of future generations. While our world is ever-changing, some experiences—like family, love, respect, illness, aging, and death—remain universal. Children need to learn to regulate their emotions, understand different perspectives,

respect others' opinions, and overcome adversity to become valuable members of society. Teaching these concepts can be challenging for parents and teachers, but books can convey these messages in accessible and relatable ways. Children are more likely to remember a story than a lesson. As an author with a teaching background, I include questions and resources at the back of my books to encourage further discussion. I want readers to reflect, relate the story to their own lives, and share similar experiences, knowing they are not alone and can find support from others.

Your journey as a writer began from a place of personal loss. How has writing these books influenced your own healing process, and what advice would you offer to others who might be considering writing as a way to cope with their grief?

Though I dreamed of becoming an author for a long time, I felt I lacked unique ideas for a good story. After experiencing loss, I encountered emotions I had never felt before. I didn't know how to cope, so I began writing to heal. Those emotions actually helped to make my writing more real and raw. I had many feelings I couldn't express verbally. It was easier to write them down than to speak, as tears would often prevent me from expressing myself clearly. Writing gave me freedom; I could cry and still get the words out. This process eventually helped me open up to friends and family. I wrote journals, stories, letters, poems, and blog posts about my experiences, sharing some while keeping others private. Each time I write, I feel a weight lifted and can move past the pain. For anyone considering writing as a way to cope with grief, my advice is to be free. Write how you feel, whatever comes to mind. Even if it's random words, just write it all down. Write about what happened, your feelings, what you wanted to say to your loved one, or what you loved or hated about them. I even created a grief journal, Creative Ways to Grieve: A Guided Grief Journal, to encourage grievers to express themselves creatively. It's not just for writing; you can draw, take photos, paint, sing, or cook—whatever you feel honors your loved one's memory.

Bridging Worlds Through Color and Canvas

Catherine Chambers weaves cultural narratives and personal stories into powerful artistic expressions that transcend geographical boundaries

In the vibrant intersection of cultural narratives and personal storytelling, Catherine Chambers emerges as a masterful chronicler of our times. Her art, deeply rooted in human connection and cross-cultural understanding, offers a fresh perspective on identity, belonging, and the threads that bind our global community.

Through her studio in London, Chambers crafts powerful visual narratives that challenge our preconceptions about culture and identity. Her work, particularly influenced by her profound connection to Ethiopia, serves as a testament to the universality of human experience – a theme that resonates throughout her diverse portfolio.

"People the world over perform the same basic activities to support their lives," Chambers reflects, discussing her observations from years of working between continents. "*My Ethiopian friends do exactly, in the setting of their environment and culture, as I do in mine.*"

Working in two distinct styles – figurative oil paintings and acrylic icon series – Chambers has developed a unique visual language that speaks to both personal and universal truths. Her oil paintings capture intimate moments laden with symbolic weight, while her triptych-format icons draw inspiration from Ethiopian Orthodox Christian tradition to tell contemporary stories.

One of her most striking pieces, "*Lying,*" currently exhibited at the National Portrait Gallery, exemplifies her ability to weave complex social commentary into seemingly simple scenes. The painting depicts a man asleep in a football shirt, touching upon themes of global consumerism and accessibility in ways that transcend geographical boundaries.

Chambers' work often challenges viewers' preconceptions, sometimes leading to surprising interpretations. She recalls an incident where a London viewer insisted that playing cards couldn't exist in Lalibela, Ethiopia – the very location where the referenced cards were purchased. Such moments of misconception fuel her creative drive to bridge cultural gaps through art.

The artist's appreciation for historical masters, particularly William Hogarth, influences her approach to social commentary. Like Hogarth's famous series "*A Rake's Progress,*" Chambers' work often follows narrative sequences that explore the consequences of human actions and decisions, particularly in cross-cultural contexts.

In an era of increasing global connectivity, Chambers' art serves as a crucial reminder of our shared humanity. Through her careful observation and masterful execution, she creates works that not only please the eye but also challenge the mind, inviting viewers to question their own assumptions about culture, identity, and human connection.

As we continue to navigate an increasingly interconnected world, Catherine Chambers' art stands as a beacon of understanding, reminding us that beneath our surface differences lie universal experiences that bind us all together. Her work isn't just about observing culture – it's about building bridges between worlds, one canvas at a time.

Artist Catherine Chambers in her London studio, where she transforms cross-cultural experiences into compelling visual narratives that challenge conventional perspectives.

"People the world over perform the same basic activities to support their lives. My Ethiopian friends do exactly, in the setting of their environment and culture, as I do in mine."

Catherine Chambers

The Paper Whisperer

A Journey Through Texture and Light Transforms Ordinary Paper into Extraordinary Art

In exclusive interview with Mosaic Digest magazine, now shared with Reader's House readers, paper artist Clare Pentlow reveals the intricate world of her unique artistic expression, where mathematics meets creativity in the most delicate of mediums.

During her Surface Pattern Design studies at University in Swansea, Wales, Clare discovered an unexpected love affair with paper that would define her artistic career. What started as a simple university project has blossomed into a distinctive artistic style characterized by her signature "fluffy-like" texture that continues to captivate audiences worldwide.

"Paper has always been my constant companion," Clare shares with Mosaic Digest. *"From folding train tickets in my pocket as a child to creating complex artistic pieces today, it's been an evolving relationship."* Her work, which now graces private collections across Europe and America, demonstrates the extraordinary potential of this humble medium.

Clare's impressive portfolio includes collaborations with luxury brands like Hermès and Lexus, and her recent appointment as an associate at the Royal Birmingham Society of Artists marks a significant milestone in her career. Working from her studio at Holyhead Studios in Coventry, she continues to push the boundaries of paper art while maintaining a strong connection to community engagement through workshops.

The artist's unique approach combines precision with organic forms, influenced by her fascination with mathematics and natural patterns. "Looking at nature under a microscope, from pollen to diatoms in water, provides endless inspiration," she explains. Her work particularly shines in its interaction with light and shadow, creating pieces that seem to dance with their environment.

What sets Clare's work apart is her methodical experimentation with paper's limitations. *"I'm constantly asking questions of the paper - how small can I cut, how many layers can I add?"* This scientific approach to artistic creation has resulted in groundbreaking techniques that challenge our perception of paper as a medium.

Despite working with prestigious brands and achieving international recognition, Clare remains committed to sharing her passion with others. "I hope people realize that paper can be more than just a surface to write on," she reflects. "It's about rediscovering the joy of creating something with your hands, away from screens and digital devices."

As paper art experiences a renaissance similar to the recent resurgence of traditional crafts like crochet and knitting, Clare stands at the forefront of this movement, proving that sometimes the most ordinary materials can yield the most extraordinary results.

For more information about Clare's workshops and upcoming exhibitions, visit her studio at Holyhead Studios, Coventry, or follow her journey on social media.

"Delicate Cellular Forms" - A mesmerizing arrangement of white paper sculptures by Clare Pentlow showcases her signature spiky formations, each piece meticulously crafted to capture light and shadow while evoking microscopic natural structures.

> *"Paper is something I've grown up with, it's something I've continually played around with."*

Clare Pentlow

Exploring the Creative Process

Janet Hennessey Dilenschneider draws inspiration from her surroundings and global events to create impactful art

Janet Hennessey Dilenschneider, a celebrated artist known for her expressionist style infused with impressionist influences, has captivated audiences worldwide with her vibrant and emotive paintings. Her latest exhibition, "Come To The Light," is a testament to her ability to convey hope and tranquility through art. In an interview conducted for Mosaic Digest, Dilenschneider shared insights into her creative process, influences, and the profound messages she aims to communicate through her work.

Dilenschneider's surroundings in Connecticut, coupled with global events, significantly impact her artistic expression. Her painting "Come To The Light" exemplifies her desire to offer peace and solace to a troubled world, providing inspiration and hope. A memorable sunrise witnessed from her window became the catalyst for this exhibition, leading her to create paintings that capture the ethereal beauty of light and sun, elements that resonate deeply with many and hold spiritual significance for some.

A pivotal moment in Dilenschneider's artistic journey occurred at the age of 16 when she encountered renowned artist Roy Lichtenstein. Initially rejected from a juried show, she was later awarded first place in Watercolor, thanks to Lichtenstein's encouragement. This experience, along with the support of a teacher who urged her to pursue art, set her on a path of artistic exploration. Her first solo show in Paris in 2013 marked a significant milestone, leading to numerous exhibitions worldwide.

Dilenschneider's expressionist style, influenced by impressionism, is characterized by free brushstrokes and vibrant colors. She aims to evoke emotions in viewers, allowing them to feel the passion and joy she experiences while painting. Her use of "simultaneous contrast," a technique borrowed from the Impressionists, creates a dynamic interplay of colors that "sing" together, adding excitement and depth to her work.

As an artist, Dilenschneider feels a personal obligation to give something meaningful to her viewers. Her paintings invite participation, encouraging viewers to find a sense of renewal and spiritual connection. She believes art can be healing and motivational, offering a respite from the chaos of the world.

In her creative process, Dilenschneider allows her "creative brain" to take over, interpreting colors and designs in unique ways. Experiences like her drive through Provence, where she was inspired by the enchanting landscapes, influence her work, resulting in paintings that capture the essence of the scenes she encounters.

Looking ahead, Dilenschneider is excited to explore new techniques and themes. She is particularly drawn to the shapes of clouds and the "misting out" of landscape scenes, aiming to capture the magical and atmospheric qualities of these subjects. Her commitment to evolving as an artist is evident in her desire to challenge her artistry and reach new heights.

Dilenschneider's passion for art was nurtured by her mother and sister, whose influence shaped her artistic style and career. She continues to apply lessons learned from them, such as the importance of contrast in both art and life.

In addition to creating beautiful art, Dilenschneider believes artists have a responsibility to comment on societal issues, such as ecology and global warming. She balances conveying these messages with creating art that provides peace and beauty, encouraging viewers to appreciate nature and develop an awareness of ecological issues.

For emerging artists, Dilenschneider advises "beating their own drum" and observing the world around them. She emphasizes the importance of learning from others while finding one's unique voice. By immersing themselves in art and allowing their "creative brain" to guide them, young artists can discover the joy and passion that define their work.

Janet Hennessey Dilenschneider's art is a beacon of light in a world often overshadowed by darkness. Her ability to inspire and uplift through her paintings is a testament to her talent and dedication to her craft. As she continues to explore new themes and techniques, her work will undoubtedly continue to resonate with audiences, offering hope and beauty to all who encounter it.

Janet Hennessey Dilenschneider is a visionary artist whose passion and dedication illuminate the art world with profound beauty.

"Art can be healing and motivational if we allow it to be."

Janet Hennessey Dilenschneider

A Journey of Art, Identity, and Connection

Sofia Ruiz, a distinguished Latin American artist hailing from San José, Costa Rica, has captivated audiences worldwide with her evocative and introspective works. Her journey into the art world began at the tender age of 16, a path shaped by personal experiences and a profound sense of longing for connection. In an interview conducted for Mosaic Digest, Ruiz shared insights into her artistic evolution, revealing how her early life experiences and academic pursuits have influenced her creative vision.

Ruiz's artistic journey was sparked by her childhood experiences, where drawing became a refuge during challenging times. Her father, often absent due to work, provided her with small notebooks and a pen to occupy her time while visiting her mother, who suffered from temporary amnesia. This period of isolation and the absence of childhood photographs deeply influenced Ruiz, driving her to explore themes of memory, identity, and psychoanalysis in her art. Her work serves as a visual diary, a healing process that continues to evolve, reflecting her quest for belonging and understanding.

In 2007, Ruiz graduated with a major in Painting and Printmaking from the School of Fine Arts in Costa Rica. These two mediums, though distinct, complement each other in her work. Printmaking, with its intricate techniques and materials, allows for careful layering of ideas, while painting offers spontaneity and raw expression. This dynamic interplay between structure and freedom is central to Ruiz's creative process, enabling her to explore complex themes with both precision and intuition.

Ruiz's artistic journey has taken her across the globe, participating in international residencies from the USA to South Korea. These experiences have enriched her understanding of art's role in diverse cultural contexts, encouraging her to experiment and blend technology with traditional printmaking. Engaging with artists from various backgrounds has broadened her perspective, allowing her to view her work through different cultural lenses and infusing her art with a global sensibility.

With over 35 exhibitions worldwide and numerous accolades, including the prestigious Best Overseas Artist Prize at the Women in Art Prize in London, Ruiz's career is marked by significant milestones. Her first solo exhibition was a pivotal moment, offering both excitement and vulnerability. Each opportunity to showcase her work, whether in a small gallery or a renowned museum, is a testament to her talent and perseverance. These experiences have bolstered her confidence, inspiring her to continue creating even in challenging times.

Beyond her artistic practice, Ruiz holds a Master's in Education, a background that profoundly influences her engagement with art. Teaching has honed her ability to simplify complex ideas, a skill that translates into her art, making intricate concepts like identity more relatable to viewers. Both teaching and creating are avenues for understanding and sharing ideas, allowing Ruiz to express them in a clearer, more accessible manner.

Through her art, Ruiz invites viewers to embark on a journey of introspection. Her exploration of themes such as fragmentation, identity, and memory encourages audiences to delve into their emotional layers, fostering a deeper understanding of their own experiences. Her work resonates universally, transcending cultural boundaries and highlighting the duality of identity—how we define ourselves versus how others perceive us. This universal theme of connection and introspection is at the heart of Ruiz's artistic vision, leaving a lasting impact on all who encounter her work.

Sofia Ruiz's art is a testament to her remarkable talent and dedication, a celebration of her journey from a young girl in Costa Rica to an internationally acclaimed artist. Her works continue to inspire and connect, offering a profound exploration of the human experience.

Exploring the profound themes of memory and identity, Sofia Ruiz's art transcends cultural boundaries and invites introspection.

Sofia Ruiz is a visionary artist whose profound exploration of identity and memory captivates and inspires audiences worldwide.

> *"Winning the Best Overseas Artist Prize at the Women in Art Prize in London was another important moment."*

Sofia Ruiz

The Influence of Heritage in Contemporary Art

Tess Jaray, renowned for her innovative abstract art, reflects on a lifelong journey through space, geometry, and color.

Portrait photo by Jack Edwards

It's not in any way deliberate that when I'm painting I set out to create space. It's all part of a process."

TESS JARAY A TRAILBLAZER IN ABSTRACT ART

Tess Jaray's work intricately combines her heritage, architectural influence, and minimalism, continuously pushing abstract art's boundaries while reshaping perceptions and nurturing new generations of artists.

TESS JARAY

ART & CULTURE

Tess Jaray has long stood as a formidable presence in the world of contemporary abstract art, with a distinguished career spanning over six decades. Her work continues to innovate and push boundaries, blending personal history with creative exploration. Born in Vienna in 1937, Jaray's early life was marked by the upheaval of World War II, leading her family to seek refuge in the United Kingdom. Her art is a reflection of this journey, intertwining her past with a forward-looking aesthetic vision.

Having studied at the prestigious Saint Martin's School of Art and the Slade School of Fine Art, Jaray established a foundation for her practice that defies simple categorization. Her art skillfully weaves together elements of Op Art, Minimalism, and Colour Field painting. Notably, Jaray became the first female lecturer at the Slade School, a significant milestone that opened doors for women in art education and inspired future generations of artists.

Jaray's public commissions have left a lasting mark on the UK's landscape, redefining spaces such as Birmingham's Centenary Square and London's Victoria Station. Her work merges art and architecture, creating environments that are both transformative and enduring.

Her paintings are known for their ability to evoke an atmosphere that feels both solid and ethereal, a product of her unique approach to space and form. Drawing inspiration from Italian Renaissance and Middle Eastern architecture, her compositions utilize vibrant color palettes and geometric motifs. These elements explore repetition and isolation

Tess Jaray, a pioneering figure in contemporary abstract art, blends vibrant colors and geometric forms to create immersive spaces that reflect her unique artistic journey and architectural influences. Her work invites viewers to explore the intricate relationship between art and the built environment, showcasing her innovative spirit and commitment to redefining abstract art.

to suggest the essence of architectural space without direct depiction. Jaray invites viewers into a world where structural lines and bold hues hint at a deeper connection between art and the built environment.

Throughout her career, Jaray has achieved prestigious recognition, with her works held in renowned collections such as the Tate,

> Tess Jaray's compositions create expansive spaces through precise geometric forms and vivid colors, echoing the architectural influences that shape her art.

the Centre Pompidou, and the Victoria and Albert Museum. Her art is celebrated for its sophistication, complexity, and capacity to reshape perceptions of abstract art.

In discussing her background, Jaray acknowledges the influence of her family's displacement from Austria due to her Jewish heritage. However, she initially sought to reject these foreign roots in favor of embracing English identity. This tension between past and present layers her work with intricate narratives of cultural identity and personal discovery. Over time, she has reconciled these aspects, allowing European musical and visual culture to permeate her art.

Jaray's exploration of geometric forms and color is not a deliberate attempt to create space but rather an integral part of her process. Through the manipulation of space, she transforms straightforward geometric elements into compelling narratives, bringing depth and interest to the canvas.

Her work in the realms of minimalism and Op Art challenges existing conventions. Jaray probes the limitations of visual non-figurative language, striving to convey as much as possible with minimal elements. This pursuit of reduction and expansion pushes the boundaries of abstract expression.

Architecture remains a core influence in Jaray's art. She translates architectural experience onto canvas by creating spaces that resonate with expression and form. Her approach considers how structures relate to their environment, mirroring the journey of painting within an artistic tradition rich with history.

As the first female art lecturer at the Slade School, Jaray has wielded influence both as an educator and an artist. Teaching at Slade offered her opportunities to connect with promising young artists, some of whom have become lifelong friends. Her trailblazing role at Slade paved the way for more female educators, highlighting the evolving landscape of art education.

Today, Tess Jaray continues to explore the potential of existing geometric forms. Rather than seeking novelty, she delves into the unexplored capacities of these forms, guided by the marks themselves. Her work remains a testament to the endless possibilities of abstraction and the profound connections between history, identity, and creative expression.

Visionary Artist Explores Identity and Belonging

"My exploration of subjects that strive for balance, without adhering to any single extreme, is deeply rooted in my personal experiences as an immigrant living in Los Angeles."

Carlos Beltran Arechiga Embodies Identity, Ambiguity, and Justice in Dynamic Contemporary Art

Carlos Beltran Arechiga's art weaves cultural narratives, environmental justice, and existential ambiguity, engaging viewers through balance, tension, and layered exploration of societal structures and personal experiences.

CARLOS BELTRAN ARECHIGA

ART & CULTURE

Carlos Beltran Arechiga is a visionary artist whose work explores themes of identity, cultural nuance, and environmental interconnectedness. His distinctive style, combining figuration and abstraction, positions him at the forefront of contemporary art. Through his dynamic creations, Arechiga delves into the spaces "in-between," urging viewers to reflect on the complexities of existence, belonging, and the structures weaving human experience.

Arechiga's journey as a painter and immigrant infuses his compositions with depth and vibrance, bridging his diverse worlds through intricate visual narratives. His canvases become both personal explorations and universal reflections, incorporating textures and materials—such as aged construction tarps—that carry historical and emotional weight. By melding organic and geometric forms, Arechiga constructs layered commentaries on balance, conflict, and harmony within a world defined by its aspirations and exclusions.

Existential Ambiguity and Artistic Process

In discussing existential ambiguity, Arechiga describes it as a central theme in his work, articulated through a deliberate formal and aesthetic in-betweenness. His backgrounds use representational structures to set mood and context, encouraging viewers to bypass the need for literal interpretation or understanding. This approach invites a visceral engagement, akin to connecting with the beauty and complexity of nature.

The artist's exploration of subjects striving for balance without adhering to extremes is deeply rooted in his personal experiences as an immigrant in Los Angeles. This unique position has guided him through a rich tapestry of cultures, languages, and identities. Arechiga's work reflects the complexities of existing between these influences, emphasizing representation nuances and quests for harmonious self-expression amidst contradictions. His paintings become spaces for contemplation and emotional resonance, encouraging viewers to introspect on their own experiences of ambiguity and balance in a multifaceted world.

Tension Between Figuration and Abstraction

Tension plays a crucial role in Arechiga's art, aiming for dynamic push-and-pull challenges that disrupt comfort levels in interpretation. Structures within his pieces are designed from varied perspectives, accommodating organic anthropomorphic forms resonating with natural structures. These interplay within sleek, hard-edged elements both complementing and contradicting the organic shapes.

> Carlos Beltran Arechiga masterfully blends abstraction and figuration, inviting introspection and dialogue on complex cultural and environmental themes through his visionary art.

The tension is thematic and formal, reflected in compositional choices incorporating marks and textures left on fabrics from previous uses, notably construction tarps involved in undocumented immigrant projects. These remnants add layers of meaning and history, fostering dialogue between past and present. Through this blending, Arechiga encourages viewers to confront perceptions of comfort and discomfort, engaging with identity, labor, and existence complexities in a self-conflicting world.

Exploration of Structures and Opportunities

Arechiga's exploration of structures underscores observation and thoughtful consideration significance, encompassing societal frameworks—policies and infrastructures dictating access, representation, education, and investment—and natural structures subject to environmental justice degradation.

For societal structures, he reflects on policies creating barriers or gateways for marginalized communities. Educational institutions can either empower individuals or reinforce inequities based on resources and accessibility. Similarly, infrastructure projects dictate investment flows into specific neighborhoods, shaping economic opportunities and community development.

Natural structures' decline from pollution and climate change affects communities disproportionately, raising social and environmental justice urgencies. For instance, low-income neighborhoods may face industrial waste impacts or lack green spaces, exposing social-environmental intersections.

Arechiga's dual perspective fosters awareness of structures' life and worldly influences, encouraging critical engagement with governing systems and natural environments for nuanced interconnectedness understanding.

Traditional "American Dream" and Disruption through Abstract Markings

Arechiga's visual language draws inspiration from sleek mid-century modern archetypes central to mass advertising campaigns promising better life conditions, albeit serving a select societal segment by ethnicity and socioeconomic status. By echoing these aesthetic forms, Arechiga critiques narratives historically marginalizing certain groups while privileging others, inviting reflection on aspirational and exclusion complexities embedded within allegedly promising structures.

Disrupting status quo marks a historical change catalyst, challenging norms to evolve societies. Through his work, Arechiga engages with this transformative idea, encouraging questioning of both visual elements and broader societal frameworks representation. He seeks to inspire dialogues about inclusive future possibilities, ensuring better living conditions and opportunities accessible beyond backgrounds.

Challenging "Promised Land" Notions

Arechiga's art challenges "promised land" concepts subtly and understatedly, not immediately apparent to viewers. His paintings use fabrics reflecting construction trade memories, highlighting overlooked worker contributions crucial to city building yet invisible in societal narratives.

These workers, often immigrants, confront systemic barriers denying them representation and recognition. The choice of materials reflecting their labor foregrounds their experiences and struggles, inviting viewers to confront prosperity-promised disparities against faced realities.

This approach serves as a societal narratives reminder surrounding labor and belonging, inviting engagement with promissory notions as nuanced realities comprising both aspiration and exclusion. Arechiga fosters interconnectedness understanding for acknowledging all societal contributors.

Dynamic Visual Experience: Gestural Markings and Structures Interplay

Through dynamic visual experiences, Arechiga aims to establish formal and conceptual interpretation frameworks fostering reflection space for diverse backgrounds. His paintings act as mirrors, inviting personal engagement contributing meanings through viewers' experiences and perspectives.

Art's true success lies in its ability to evoke viewer change, even momentarily, within minds or hearts. Such fleeting connections serve as powerful change catalysts, triggering lingering thoughts and emotions beyond initial viewing. Arechiga sees these moments as significant, influencing daily life and perceptions, fostering awareness and deeper shared human experiences.

By encouraging introspection, Arechiga hopes to inspire dialogues extending beyond his artwork, for ongoing reflections and world engagement.

Crafting Dreams and Dualities in Modern Art

Artist Brian Hubble blends fine detail with surreal, expressive imagery, using image-transfer techniques to create pieces that explore the relationship between images, performance, and the unexpected. His work invites contemplation through poetic contrasts.

DANIEL CERREJON

A DIALOGUE THROUGH DRAWING USING A RANGE OF MATERIALS

Editors Desk

"

> The knots are made by tying one after another in a compulsive manner until the rope can no longer be folded."

Daniel Cerrejon is a visionary artist whose work challenges the boundaries between the tangible and the abstract, the personal and the universal. With a career that spans continents and artistic disciplines, Cerrejon has cultivated a practice that is as intellectually rigorous as it is emotionally resonant. His art delves into the intersections of data, objects, and the human body, transforming cold, statistical abstractions into visceral, poetic forms. From his CORPUS series, which reimagines bodily measurements as intricate knots imbued with warmth and humanity, to his exploration of proxemics and relational distances, Cerrejon's work invites viewers to reconsider the ways in which we perceive ourselves and the spaces we inhabit. His ability to balance the technical with the corporeal, the conceptual with the sensory, marks him as a singular voice in contemporary art.

In this interview, Cerrejon offers a rare glimpse into his creative process and the philosophies that underpin his practice. From his early studies in Madrid and New York to his time at the Whitney Independent Study Program, he reflects on the cultural and intellectual influences that have shaped his journey. Through his thoughtful responses, Cerrejon unpacks the layers of meaning in his work, revealing how he transforms data into art and abstraction into intimacy. This conversation is a testament to his profound ability to bridge the gap between the empirical and the emotional, creating art that not only engages the mind but also resonates deeply with the soul.

In the CORPUS series, what significance do the knots and

ART & CULTURE

An abstract representation of connection and preservation, featuring an organic form encased in transparent plastic, symbolizing the delicate balance of human interaction and containment.

flesh-like tones hold in relation to the "cold" statistical language used in the titles?

Each piece in the CORPUS series consists of various components. To answer your question, we can focus on four: the knots, color, titles, and bodily measurements. I appreciate how you frame your question in terms of 'coldness.' To me, two of these components are 'cold'—the measurements and color—while the other two, the knots and titles, feel 'warm.' By 'cold,' I mean purely conceptual elements lacking traditional artistry. The measurements represent body data, while the color comes from covering the knots with makeup in a shade that approximates the average skin tone of the American population at the time the works were made. Each piece in the CORPUS series reflects 'the average American person,' as indicated by the titles.

Daniel Cerrejon masterfully bridges the technical and the emotional, creating art that transforms data into deeply human experiences.

The two elements I consider 'warm,' as opposed to the 'cold' ones, are the knots and titles. Each title in this series combines various standard bodily measurements, arranged in a poetic way. The rules for these poetic titles vary for each piece. Sometimes, the poetry lies in the sound and rhythm of the words, while other times, it emerges from the sequential meaning of specific measurements. An example title from this series is From One Hand to the Other, whilst Each Holds the Other, of the Average American Person.

The last of the four elements we're discussing is the knot, which I described as a 'warm' element in this temperature analogy. Each knot is made by cutting a rope to the length specified in the title and tying it into a continuous knot without a beginning or end. The process of knotting is arbitrary and emotional, created by tying one knot after another in a compulsive manner until the rope can no longer be folded.

Your work brings a visceral, almost tangible presence to abstract measurements. How do you balance the contrast between the technical and the corporeal in your art?

My artwork is the embodiment of data, often related to our bodies, into physical objects. This process involves a back-and-forth between a scientific approach—an empirical method of acquiring knowledge —and an artistic approach, which is more intuitive in solving and understanding a situation. As we discussed, some works begin with a system of bodily measurements. These measurements transform into language, which is articulated in a specific way, and this language, in turn, influences the form of the work. This form is then received by the viewer, shifting their perception of themselves. It is in this final stage, when the work is perceived, that I would describe the experience as visceral. Not only because some pieces resemble guts or internal organs, evoking raw, physical sensations, but also because the perception of objects appeals to physical sensations rather than logical reasoning. I believe this sensory engagement shapes how we understand ourselves. It's not just in artworks; all the objects around us play a role in shaping our self-perception.

Could you share more about your exploration of proxemics in your work? How do you approach representing human relational distances through sculpture?

Proxemics is the study of how people use space and distance in communication, and how these distances can convey meanings, emotions, and social dynamics. In my work, I explore these 'empty distances'—the spaces between people interacting—and transform them into objects. The resulting objects serve as index of an absence.

How does the concept of "average" influence your art, particularly in terms of bodily metrics and flesh tones, and what commentary are you hoping to make on standardization?

I became interested in the concept of the average because it transforms something universal into something particular. The data tables I use in my work are already the result of averaging—data taken from a large group of people within a specific segment of the population, with the average presented as a universal. In my work, I often reverse this process, calculating the average of various universal data points to produce a singular value, which then becomes an art object. The average calculation explores the relationship between the universal and the particular, or the collective and the individual.

By using this averaging method, I break the typical logic of data extraction. While averaging is normally part of data analysis, in my work it serves no practical purpose other than to create art.

For viewers of your work, what emotions or reactions do you hope to evoke as they encounter the embodied and recontextualized measurements in your sculptures?

As I mentioned before, more than emotions or reactions, I'm interested in art and the act of making because of how our surroundings influence our perception of ourselves .Making art is a way for me to engage with the constellation of things around us.

"Vulnerability, 2020: A striking composition of contrasts, this image captures the delicate balance between strength and fragility, as a figure crouches gracefully against a warm, rust-colored backdrop, adorned with symbolic elements."

Redefining Art and Identity

HAN YANG

Discover how Han Yang blends ancient philosophies with modern technology to redefine femininity and identity

as told to Archie Preston

Han Yang explores metaphysical nothingness and posthumanism, blending ancient and modern elements to challenge traditional gender narratives and redefine identity through her innovative art and photography.

Han Yang, a visionary artist and fine art photographer, graced the cover of WOWwART, an art magazine of NewYox Media, bringing with her a profound exploration of art that challenges the very fabric of traditional aesthetics. Her work is a testament to the power of art to transcend boundaries and redefine norms, as she delves into the metaphysical realm of nothingness—a concept that has not only fueled her intellectual curiosity but also formed the foundation of her groundbreaking dissertations.

Han Yang's artistic journey is a harmonious blend of empirical life experiences and the timeless principles of Buddhist philosophy, expressed through a diverse array of multimedia forms. Her unique ability to visually articulate metaphysical nothingness is a hallmark of her innovative spirit, echoing the essence of ancient Zen paintings while simultaneously pushing the envelope of contemporary art.

In her photography, Han Yang masterfully intertwines themes of femininity, the human body, and technology with oriental metaphors, challenging and expanding traditional gender narratives. By integrating elements of Chinese culture with futuristic imagery, she reimagines femininity as powerful and autonomous, creating a visual dialogue that transcends cultural boundaries and redefines identity in a modern context.

Her research on posthumanism further enriches her artistic practice, allowing her to explore identity and gender through a nonhuman lens. By merging human and mechanical elements, Han Yang dissolves conventional boundaries, promoting a vision of identity that is fluid, interconnected, and liberated from traditional constraints.

Han Yang's creative process is a journey into the psychological depths of her subjects, capturing their inner worlds with a delicate balance of abstract and surreal elements. Her work navigates the intersection of commercial fashion photography and personal conceptual exploration, seamlessly blending artistic expression with market demands.

Recognized with prestigious accolades such as the SONY Young Photographer Award and the World's Top 10 Women Photographers Contest, Han Yang's career is a testament to her relentless pursuit of innovation and boundary-pushing artistry. As she continues her PhD at King's College London, her academic research and visual art practice intertwine, drawing inspiration from posthumanist and gender studies to create visual narratives that challenge and inspire.

Han Yang's work is not just art; it is a profound exploration of identity, technology, and the human condition, inviting us all to see the world through a lens of infinite possibilities.

Your work often intertwines themes of femininity, the human body, and technology with oriental metaphors. How do you use these metaphors to challenge or enhance traditional narratives of gender in your photography?

Continued *on page 66*

 **Continued** *from page 65*

PAPAVER ROSES

A whimsical dreamscape unfolds as a figure in a fluffy pink garment interacts with oversized flowers, creating an ethereal atmosphere that blurs the line between fashion and nature.

INVISIBLE, 2020

An evocative exploration of presence and absence, 'Invisible, 2020' captures the essence of what is seen and unseen, inviting viewers to ponder the hidden layers of reality.

In my photography, I use oriental metaphors to challenge and expand traditional gender narratives by incorporating elements of Chinese culture into contemporary representations of femininity. I often draw on cultural symbols like ancient Chinese script, mythical creatures, and traditional garments, which embody strength, transformation, and resilience. These symbols serve as a foundation for reinterpreting femininity in a modern context.

By combining these symbols with futuristic and technological imagery, I aim to portray women as powerful and autonomous, moving away from conventional passive depictions. Technology, in my work, symbolizes evolution—indicating that gender and identity are not static, but rather fluid and ever-changing. The juxtaposition of ancient and modern elements creates a visual conversation that not only transcends cultural boundaries but also redefines femininity in a way that harmonizes tradition with progress.

You're currently conducting research on posthumanism, particularly exploring gender through a nonhuman perspective in photography. How does this research inform your artistic practice, and how do you envision posthuman concepts reshaping our understanding of identity and gender in art?

My research on posthumanism informs my artistic practice by allowing me to challenge conventional notions of identity and gender. Posthumanism extends the concept of the "self" beyond human limitations, embracing the influence of technology, artificial intelligence, and the environment on identity formation. In my photography, I often merge human bodies with mechanical or abstract elements, dissolving the boundaries of gender and biological traits. This exploration of nonhuman perspectives highlights gender as fluid and evolving, rather than binary or fixed. I envision posthuman concepts reshaping art by promoting identities that are hybrid, interconnected, and no longer defined by traditional physical or social constraints, allowing for more inclusive and expansive representations of the self.

Your photography combines abstract and surreal elements with rich, delicate emotions. Can you walk us through your creative process and how you capture the psychological depth and inner

Han Yang is a visionary artist whose work transcends boundaries, redefining identity and challenging traditional narratives with profound innovation.

world of the characters you portray?

My creative process begins with understanding the emotional core of the concept or subject I'm working with. I spend time reflecting on the psychological nuances I want to evoke, whether it's vulnerability, strength, or transformation. From there, I incorporate abstract and surreal elements to create a visual language that mirrors these emotions without being bound by realism. I often use lighting, color, and unconventional angles to suggest an altered or dream-like reality, allowing the viewer to step into the internal world of the character. During the shoot, I work closely with the model, encouraging them to channel specific emotions, which helps bring out a raw, authentic expression. The delicate balance between surreal imagery and emotional depth is where I believe the psychological richness of my work emerges.

As both an artist and a fine art photographer, how do you navigate the balance between fashion photography's commercial aspects and your more personal, conceptual explorations of gender and the human body?

Navigating between the commercial nature of fashion photography and my personal conceptual work requires a constant balancing act. In fashion photography, the visual language often needs to align with brand identity and market trends, which can sometimes feel limiting.

However, I see this as an opportunity to bring my own voice into commercial projects by subtly weaving in themes of gender fluidity and the human body's complexities. When working on personal projects, I have the freedom to fully explore these concepts without constraints, diving deeper into abstract interpretations of identity and embodiment. I strive to find intersections where the artistic and commercial worlds can coexist, creating images that not only fulfil commercial needs but also provoke thought and emotion, allowing both worlds to inform and enrich each other.

You've been recognized with prestigious awards like the SONY Young Photographer Award and the World's Top 10 Women Photographers Contest. How have these accolades influenced your career, and what role do you see awards playing in the development of your artistic voice?

Receiving awards such as the SONY Young Photographer Award and recognition in the World's Top 10 Women Photographers Contest has greatly influenced my exploration of gender, identity, creativity, and technology. These accolades have given me the platform to delve deeper into these themes, allowing me to continue challenging traditional narratives around gender and identity through my work. They have affirmed my artistic direction and opened new pathways for creative collaborations where I can further merge technology with the human form. While awards are not the only validation, they play an important role in providing the space and recognition to push boundaries and experiment more freely, encouraging me to expand my exploration of posthumanism, fluidity, and innovation in both photography and art.

As you pursue your PhD at King's College London, how do you integrate your academic research with your visual art practice? Are there any particular philosophical or theoretical concepts that have recently inspired your work?

My PhD research has deeply informed and enriched my visual art practice. I explore the intersections of posthumanism, gender studies, and identity, drawing heavily from theoretical frameworks that challenge human-centric perspectives. Concepts such as Donna Haraway's cyborg theory and Rosi Braidotti's posthuman subjectivity have particularly inspired me to think beyond traditional representations of the body. These ideas resonate in my photography, where I often merge organic and mechanical elements to represent fluidity in identity and gender. The academic environment allows me to critically engage with these philosophical discourses and translate them into visual narratives. My research also helps me push the boundaries of how technology, the human form, and identity interact, making both my scholarly and artistic work extensions of each other.

J"In my photography, I use oriental metaphors to challenge and expand traditional gender narratives."
– Yang

The Bold Messages Behind Barbie and Lenticular Art

CECILE PLAISANCE

Cecile Plaisance's photography celebrates femininity and freedom, challenges societal norms, and uses Barbie dolls to provoke thought on female autonomy and beauty.

CECILE PLAISANCE'S ARTISTRY CELEBRATES FEMININITY AND FREEDOM THROUGH PROVOCATIVE EXPRESSION

as told to Archie Preston

Cecile Plaisance's artistic voyage is a daring and unapologetic celebration of femininity, freedom, and provocative expression. Once immersed in the rigorous world of European financial markets, Plaisance transitioned into photography, a medium through which she fearlessly explores themes of gender, societal expectations, and the constraints imposed by religion. Her imaginative use of Barbie dolls challenges traditional perceptions of beauty and identity, transforming these iconic figures into symbols of female autonomy. Her distinct visual style, a harmonious blend of playful imagery and serious commentary, invites introspection on the societal constructs shaping women's lives.

Plaisance's photographs transcend their immediate allure, resonating with themes that provoke thought and dialogue. Her series, such as "Fuck the Rules," and her innovative lenticular prints weave narratives of rebellion and empowerment. Drawing inspiration from luminaries like Helmut Newton and Ellen von Unwerth, Plaisance lends her unique voice to elevate conversations about femininity, using beauty, humor, and defiance in captivating forms. Her artworks, often a provocative mix of provocativeness and profundity, challenge societal norms and open spaces for women to unapologetically embrace their freedoms.

Cecile Plaisance masterfully uses playfulness with profound feminist statements, delivering bold, provocative art that champions women's empowerment.

The Unexpected Artistic Path: From Finance to Photography

Plaisance's background in economics and finance played a minimal role in influencing her artistic journey. From a young age, she was enthralled by images of women in magazines, a fascination that transcended into her adult life. Upon exiting the financial world, she embarked on a new adventure without knowing where it would lead. The transition marked a complete departure into a realm where she could explore and depict the transcendental beauty of women—an endeavor she is passionate about.

Embracing Barbie as a Medium of Feminist Expression

The shift from capturing travel scenes and objects to focusing on Barbie dolls was a natural progression for Plaisance. Her passion for photography has been longstanding, significantly since the birth of her children. It wasn't until her time in photography school, when a free-themed exhibition allowed her to pay homage to Helmut Newton, that Barbie came into focus. With numerous dolls at her disposal, this became both a nostalgic nod to her childhood and a humorous engagement with feminist themes. Through Barbie, Plaisance proposes that femininity can be both a playful and provocative domain for feminist expression, challenging preconceived notions of feminism.

A Balance of Playfulness and Provocation

For Plaisance, balancing the playful and provocative elements of her Barbie-centric images is essential in conveying deeper messages about femininity and women's rights. She advocates for gender equality but insists that women should not abandon their femininity. The freedom for women to dress as they please, to embrace beauty, and to exercise choice in self-expression are central rights. Plaisance uses her Barbie's ultra-feminine form to underscore these rights, rejecting societal and religious dictates that restrict women's freedom and movement. In her work, the provocation serves as a powerful tool to amplify her messages.

Unveiling Female Autonomy through Provocative Imagery

The decision to undress Barbies in her art is deliberate, illustrating that in a liberated world, a woman should have the autonomy to choose how she presents her body. This statement critiques the religious laws in specific regions that render women invisible and subordinate. Plaisance's work is a call to challenge these outdated norms and support women's autonomy and visibility.

Evolving Artistry: From Barbies to Human Models

Now working with human models, Plaisance continues her advocacy for women's freedom. The process with human models differs as it becomes a collaborative engagement, where ideas and support for her project are mutual. Models, like Marisa Papen, push boundaries further, embracing a lifestyle of freedom that resonates with Plaisance's artistic vision. The exchange with human subjects enriches her work far more than her previous endeavors with Barbies.

The Allure of Lenticular Prints

Plaisance employs lenticular prints to enhance the viewer's experience, adding a dynamic and interactive element to her art. This medium, reminiscent of childhood nostalgia with its shifting images, acts as a "car stopper," compelling people to engage with her work. Through pieces like "Fuck the Rules," Plaisance delivers strong, explicit messages—depictions of rebellion against constricting cultural and religious norms. Her work, bold and thought-provoking, reaffirms her dedication to advocating for women's liberation and autonomy.

Cecile Plaisance remains a formidable force in contemporary art, her work inviting viewers to reexamine and celebrate the multifaceted nature of femininity.

Available in

PRINT

Americas to Australia

Europe to Africa Reader's House is available over 190 countries and thousands of retaiers, platforms including Amazon, Barnes & Noble, Walmart, Waterstone's .....

ELECTRONIC

It is an electronic (flip book) format and interactive. Accessable from electronic devices like pc, smart phone, notepads..

ONLINE

All interviews, we conduct make them accessable online for free.

SOCIAL MEDIA

We are on Facebook, Instagram and X. Please follow us on social media @readershousemag

contact us today for an interview opportunity at editor@readershouse.co.uk

Subscribe Now!

YES! I would like a subscription to

- ☐ Current Issue for ☐ Includes Shipping and Handling
- ☐ One-Year Subscription (_____ Issues) for
- ☐ Two-Year Subscription (_____ Issues) for

☐ I am a renewing a current subscription ☐ I am a new subscriber

Name: ______________________ Phone: ______________

Shipping Address: ______________________

Billing Address: ______________________

Email: ______________________

☐ Yes, I would like to receive updates, newsletters and special offers

☐ No, I would NOT like to receive updates, newsletters and special offers

Payment Type: ☐ Cash ☐ Check

Please mail this form to:

Magazine Name: *Reader's House* by Newyox 200 Suite, 134-146 Curtain Road EC2A 3AR London readershouse.co.uk

www.ingramcontent.com/pod-product-compliance
Lightning Source LLC
Chambersburg PA
CBHW041205100726
47911CB00016B/871

* 9 7 8 1 6 4 2 2 6 4 2 8 9 *